Law and Gospel

The Lutheran Difference Series

Korey Maas

Contributions by

Robert C. Baker

CONCORDIA PUBLISHING HOUSE · SAINT LOUIS

Copyright © 2005 by Concordia Publishing House
3558 S. Jefferson Ave.
St. Louis, MO 63118-3968
1-800-325-3040 • www.cph.org

Written by Korey Maas

Edited by Robert C. Baker

Scripture quotations are from The Holy Bible, English Standard Version, copyright © 2001 by Crossway Bibles, a division of Good News Publishers. Used by permission. All rights reserved.

Quotations from the Lutheran Confessions are taken from the *Concordia Triglotta,* © 1921 Concordia Publishing House.

This publication may be available in braille, in large print, or on cassette tape for the visually impaired. Please allow 8 to 12 weeks for delivery. Write to the Library for the Blind, 7550 Watson Rd., St. Louis, MO 63119-4409; call toll-free 1-888-215-2455; or visit the Web site: www.blindmission.org.

Manufactured in the U.S.A.

1 2 3 4 5 6 7 8 9 10   14 13 12 11 10 09 08 07 06 05

Contents

About This Series

"I just don't get it."

"What's that?"

"You Lutherans say you believe in the Ten Commandments, but you worship on Sunday, not the Jewish Sabbath."

"But Jesus is our Sabbath rest."

"So, the Third Commandment no longer applies?"

As Lutherans interact with other Christians, they often find themselves struggling to explain their beliefs and practices. Although many Lutherans have learned the "what" of the doctrines of the church, they do not always have a full scriptural foundation to share the "why." When confronted with different doctrines, they cannot clearly state their faith, much less understand the differences.

Because of insecurities about explaining particular doctrines or practices, some Lutherans may avoid opportunities to share what they have learned from Christ and His Word. The Lutheran Difference Bible study series will identify how Lutherans differ from other Christians and show from the Bible why Lutherans differ. These studies will prepare Lutherans to share their faith and help non-Lutherans understand the Lutheran difference.

Student Introduction

With characteristic boldness Luther once defined the content of the Christian faith by saying, "Theology's proper subject is man guilty of sin and condemned, and God his Justifier and Savior." Though brief and provocative, it is not a rash statement. Luther, who was by vocation a professor of the Bible, understood well that theology—words about God—has its only sure foundation in Scripture, the Word *of* God. As his years of study continually made evident, the great subject of Scripture itself is man as sinner and God as Savior.

By his own admission, however, Luther did not always understand the content of Scripture. As a young monk he was acutely aware of what it had to say about his own sin and well-deserved condemnation, but he knew little of its comforting doctrine of God the Justifier and Savior. This he only came to know once he had learned to distinguish between Scripture's two main themes. As Luther stated, "When I understood the proper distinction—that the Law is one thing and that the Gospel is another—then I broke through."

For Luther, a proper distinction between Law and Gospel opened the door to a right understanding of God's Word and, therefore, a right understanding of God's will for humankind and our salvation. Throughout its history, the Lutheran church has continued to maintain that rightly distinguishing between Law and Gospel is absolutely necessary in this regard. The Law shows us God's will and reveals our sin; the Gospel proclaims our salvation in Christ. To confuse these two doctrines is to remain confused about ourselves and about our God. To misunderstand them is to misunderstand the reason for the incarnation, life, death, and resurrection of Christ. In short, Law and Gospel are the means by which we can rightly understand the whole of the Christian faith.

This is, of course, not an easy task. Luther himself realized that no one can perfect the art of properly distinguishing between these two biblical doctrines. But in light of their great importance, he also encouraged Christians to exercise daily in this task. "If anyone knows this art well," he said, speaking equally of pastors, professors, and parishioners, "he deserves to be called a theologian."

An Overview of Christian Denominations

The following outline of Christian history will help you understand where the different denominations come from and how they are related to one another. Use this outline in connection with the "Comparisons" sections found throughout the study. Statements of belief for the different churches are drawn from their official confessional writings.

The Great Schism

Eastern Orthodox: On July 16, 1054, Cardinal Humbert entered the Cathedral of the Holy Wisdom in Constantinople just before the worship service. He stepped to the altar and left a letter condemning Michael Cerularius, patriarch of Constantinople. Cerularius responded by condemning the letter and its authors. In that moment, Christian churches of the east and west were severed from each other. Their disagreements centered on what bread could be used in the Lord's Supper and the addition of the filioque statement to the Nicene Creed.

The Reformation

Lutheran: On June 15, 1520, Pope Leo X wrote a letter condemning Dr. Martin Luther for his Ninety-five Theses. Luther's theses had challenged the sale of indulgences, a fund-raising effort to pay for the building of St. Peter's Cathedral in Rome. The letter charged Luther with heresy and threatened to excommunicate him if he did not retract his writings within 60 days. Luther replied by publicly burning the letter. Leo excommunicated him on January 3, 1521, and condemned all who agreed with Luther or supported his cause.

Reformed: In 1522 the preaching of Ulrich Zwingli in Zurich, Switzerland, convinced people to break their traditional Lenten fast. Also, Zwingli preached that priests should be allowed to marry. When local friars challenged these departures from medieval church practice, the Zurich Council supported Zwingli and agreed that the Bible should guide Christian doctrine and practice. Churches of the Reformed tradition include Presbyterians and Episcopalians.

Anabaptist: In January 1525 Conrad Grebel, a follower of Ulrich Zwingli, rebaptized Georg Blaurock. Blaurock began rebaptizing others and founded the Swiss Brethren. Their insistence on adult believers' Baptism distinguished them from other churches of the Reformation. Anabaptists attracted social extremists who advocated violence in the cause of Christ, complete pacifism, or communal living. Mennonite, Brethren, and Amish churches descend from this movement.

The Counter Reformation

Roman Catholic: When people call the medieval church "Roman Catholic," they make a common historical mistake. Roman Catholicism as we know it emerged after the Reformation. As early as 1518 Luther and other reformers had appealed to the pope and requested a council to settle the issue of indulgences. Their requests were hindered or denied for a variety of theological and political reasons. Finally, on December 13, 1545, 34 leaders from the churches who opposed the Reformation gathered at the invitation of Pope Paul III. They began the Council of Trent (1545–63), which established the doctrine and practice of Roman Catholicism.

Post-Reformation Movements

Baptist: In 1608 or 1609 John Smyth, a former pastor of the Church of England, baptized himself by pouring water over his head. He formed a congregation of English Separatists in Holland, who opposed the rule of bishops and infant Baptism. This marked the start of the English Baptist churches, which remain divided doctrinally over the theology of John Calvin (Particular Baptists) and Jacob Arminius (General Baptists). In the 1800s the Restoration Movement of Alexander Campbell, a former Presbyterian minister, adopted many Baptist teachings. These churches include the Disciples of Christ (Christian Churches) and the Churches of Christ.

Wesleyan: In 1729 John and Charles Wesley gathered with three other men to study the Scripture, receive Communion, and discipline one another according to the "method" laid down in the Bible. Later, John Wesley's preaching caused religious revivals in England and America. Methodists, Wesleyans, Nazarenes, and Pentecostals form the Wesleyan family of churches.

Liberal: In 1799 Friedrich Schleiermacher published *Addresses on Religion* in an attempt to make Christianity appealing to people influenced by rationalism. He argued that religion is not a body of doctrines, provable truths, or a system of ethics, but belongs to the realm of feelings. His ideas did not lead to the formation of a new denomination, but deeply influenced Christian thinking. Denominations most thoroughly affected by liberalism are the United Church of Christ, Disciples of Christ, and Unitarianism.

Lutheran Facts

All who worship the Holy Trinity and trust in Jesus Christ for the forgiveness of sins are regarded by Lutherans as fellow Christians, despite denominational differences.

Lutheran churches first described themselves as *evangelische* or evangelical churches. Opponents of these churches called them *Lutheran* after Dr. Martin Luther, the sixteenth-century German church reformer.

Lutherans are not disciples of Dr. Martin Luther but disciples of Jesus Christ. They proudly accept the name Lutheran because they agree with Dr. Luther's teaching from the Bible, as summarized in Luther's Small Catechism.

Although all Christian churches use Holy Scripture, Lutherans emphasize that Scripture is the final and only certain judge of doctrine and practice (*sola scriptura*)—not human traditions, reason, or churchly authority.

Lutherans also confess the three ecumenical creeds (Apostles', Nicene, and Athanasian) because they correctly summarize biblical teaching.

Lutherans find that distinguishing Law and Gospel is a key interpretive principle in understanding the Bible (see John 1:17; 2 Corinthians 3:6), particularly how sinners are justified before God by His grace through faith in Christ (see John 3:16–17; Galatians 4:4–5; Hebrews 2:14–17; 1 Timothy 1:15).

Lutherans believe that the proper application of Law and Gospel is imperative, so that sinners are brought to repentance through the condemnation of the Law and are justified through faith in the promises of the Gospel.

The confusion of Law and Gospel leaves one between Scylla and Charybdis: either self-righteous or with weakened faith. Such confusion confirms unrepentant sinners in their sinful thoughts, words, and deeds, and starves repentant sinners of God's free forgiveness through Christ's life, death, and resurrection.

To prepare for "God's Word: The Law," read Psalm 119:1–16.

God's Word: The Law

In a madhouse there exists no law.

—John Clare

If we are in a great hurry, we may not appreciate traffic laws. If we are buying a home or opening a business, we may dislike existing zoning laws. Rules and regulations can sometimes seem highly inconvenient. Most people, however, recognize their importance. In fact, every society in the world has some form of law, some code of right and wrong. Without laws the world would become a madhouse.

1. What laws do you most frequently find inconvenient? Can you think of a good reason for the existence of these laws? What consequences would result if they were repealed?

Holy Legality

2. Read Ephesians 5:15–17; Psalm 40:8; and Romans 7:12. With what do the Old and New Testament writers associate the Law of God? How does Scripture therefore describe this Law?

3. Compare Exodus 31:18 and Romans 2:14–15. Who is able to know God's Law? In what different ways do people come to know the Law?

4. Read and compare Ecclesiastes 7:20; 1 John 3:4; and James 2:10. Though all people are conscious of the Law, what do these passages say about our ability to keep the Law?

5. Read 1 Timothy 1:8–11. What is one of the uses for which God's Law has been given?

6. Compare Romans 3:20 and Romans 7:7. What is a second use for which God's Law has been given?

7. The Word of God not only warns against and reveals sin; it also clearly states the consequences of sin. Read Deuteronomy 27:26 and Romans 6:23. How serious are the consequences for breaking God's Law?

8. The Law of God may be used in different ways. There is one thing, however, for which the Law is not to be used. Compare Galatians 3:10–11 and Galatians 5:4. What does God not intend His Law to do?

Crime and Punishment

If our civil laws can at times seem burdensome, the divine Law of God can seem even more so! No one escapes its jurisdiction. No one escapes accusation for breaking this Law. And, if we were left to our own devices, no one would escape its penalties.

9. As you meditate on the Law of God—its nature, use, and consequences—what effects does it have on you? What emotions or reactions does the Law produce?

10. Read Galatians 3:13. Remembering what the Law can and cannot do, what comfort does Paul offer those who have not kept God's Law?

Utter Silence

Paul informs us that the Law speaks "so that every mouth may be stopped, and the whole world may be held accountable to God" (Romans 3:19)—*every* mouth, the *whole* world. Though every society throughout the world has some form of law, not all people recognize the Law of the God who created this world.

11. Reread Romans 2:14–15. As you encounter those who do not know or do not believe the Bible, consider how you might begin to discuss both Law and Gospel with them.

Comparisons

Eastern Orthodox: "What is necessary in order to please God and to save one's own soul? In the first place, a knowledge of the true God, and a right faith in Him; in the second place, a life according to faith, and good works" (*The Longer Catechism of the Eastern Church*, question 3).

Lutheran: "We believe, teach, and confess that the Law is properly a divine doctrine, which teaches what is right and pleasing to God, and reproves everything that is sin and contrary to God's will. For this reason, then, everything that reproves sin is, and belongs to, the preaching of the Law" (Epitome of the Formula of Concord V 2–3).

Reformed/Presbyterian: "God gave to Adam a law, as a covenant of works, by which He bound him and all his posterity to personal, entire, exact, and perpetual obedience; promised life upon the fulfilling, and threatened death upon the breach of it; and endued him with power and ability to keep it. . . . Although true believers be not under the law as a covenant of works, to be thereby justified or condemned; yet is it of great use to them, as well as to others" (*The Westminster Confession of Faith*, ch. 19.1, 6).

Roman Catholic: "The holy Synod declares first, that, for the correct and sound understanding of the doctrine of Justification, it is necessary that each one recognize and confess, that, whereas all men had lost their innocence in the prevarication of Adam . . . free-will, attenuated as it was in its powers, and bent down, was by no means extinguished in them" (*The Canons and Decrees of the Council of Trent*, Session 6, Decree on Justification).

Baptist: "We believe that man was created in holiness, under the law of his Maker; but by voluntary transgression fell from that holy and happy state; in consequence of which all mankind are now sinners, not by constraint, but choice; being by nature utterly void of that holiness required by the law of God, positively inclined to evil; and therefore under just condemnation to eternal ruin, without defense or excuse" (*The New Hampshire Baptist Confession*, article 3).

Wesleyan/Methodist: "Although the law given from God by Moses, as touching ceremonies and rites, does not bind Christians, nor ought the civil precepts thereof of necessity be received in any commonwealth, yet, notwithstanding, no Christian whatsoever is free from the obedience of the commandments which are called moral" (*Methodist Articles of Religion*, article 6).

Liberal: "We cannot define Christian ethics in terms of a church-controlled society. Neither can we regard Christian duty as identical with biblical precepts. . . . Christian ethics should be defined as the determination of the duties of a modern Christian living in the modern world. To define it in terms of an ethical system belonging to another age is to fail to make Christianity ethical" (Gerald Birney Smith in *A Guide to the Study of the Christian Religion*, p. 570).

Point to Remember

I desire to do Your will, O my God; Your law is within my heart. Psalm 40:8

To prepare for "God's Word: The Gospel," read 1 Corinthians 15:1–4.

God's Word: The Gospel

Ill news hath wings, and with the wind doth go,
Comfort's a cripple and comes ever slow.

—Michael Drayton

War, famine, crime, scandal: such is the stuff of headlines. It grabs our attention; it sells newspapers. And it depresses us. There is, to be sure, a desperate shortage of good news in our daily news. So much so that we are frequently skeptical of good news; in moments of cynicism we may even be tempted to label it sentimentalism rather than proper news.

12. What was the last bit of good news you read in the newspaper, saw on television, or heard on the radio? What was the last bit of good news that had relevance for your own life?

Power Points

13. Read Romans 1:16–17. How does Paul famously describe the Gospel? In what way does it differ from the Law?

14. In the above passage, Paul mentions righteousness being "revealed" with the Gospel. Compare Ephesians 6:19 and 2 Corinthians 4:4. How do these passages shed light on why the Gospel must be revealed?

15. Scripture declares that God's Law is universal; it is given to all people. Read 1 Timothy 2:3–6 and 2 Peter 3:9. For whom is the Gospel revealed?

16. Compare Mark 1:1; 2 Corinthians 2:12; and Romans 16:25–27. What fuller names or descriptions do these passages give to the Gospel? What significance do these have for understanding the Gospel?

17. Sadly, many people and many religions preach about Christ without in fact preaching the Gospel. Read 1 Corinthians 15:1–4 and compare 1 Corinthians 2:2. What does Paul say forms the content of the true Gospel message?

18. Read Galatians 1:6–8. What warning does Paul here give? Why is he so adamant that the church reject all other "gospels"?

Living by Faith

In the same way that many people faithfully read the morning paper or turn on the evening news, Christians are eager to hear important news that affects their lives. There is none more important or more relevant than the good news of Christ Himself.

19. In the light of question 14, what relevance does frequent worship have for the Christian?

20. In the light of questions 17 and 18 above, what benefits may the Christian derive from frequent study of God's Word and sound Christian doctrine?

Communicating the Message

In our sinful world, where good news is so infrequently heard, it is easy to become skeptical about such news or cynical about its content. But our Lord assures us that His Gospel is no sentimental story; it is true, faithfully reported, and eternally relevant. It is good news indeed.

21. How might you respond to a friend who believes the Gospel is too good to be true?

22. How might you respond to a friend who believes that the importance of Jesus is found in His moral example rather than in His death and resurrection?

Comparisons

Eastern Orthodox: "What was Christ's doctrine? The Gospel of the kingdom of God, or, in other words, the doctrine of salvation and eternal happiness, the same that is now taught in the Orthodox Church (Mark 1:14–15). How have we salvation by Christ's doctrine? When we receive it with all our heart, and walk according to it. For, as the lying words of the devil, received by our first parents, became in them the seed of sin and death; so, on the contrary the true Word of Christ, heartily received by Christians, becomes in them the seed of a holy and immortal life

17

(1 Peter 1:23). How have we salvation by Christ's life? When we imitate it. For He says, 'If anyone serves Me, let him follow Me; and where I am, there shall also My servant be' (John 12:26)" (*The Longer Catechism of the Eastern Church*, questions 196–98).

Lutheran: "But the Gospel is properly such a doctrine as teaches what man who has not observed the Law of God, and therefore is condemned by it, is to believe, namely, that Christ has expiated and made satisfaction for all his sins, and has obtained and acquired for him, without any merit of his . . . forgiveness of sins, righteousness that avails before God, and eternal life" (Epitome of the Formula of Concord V 4).

Reformed/Presbyterian: "Elect infants, dying in infancy, are regenerated and saved by Christ through the Spirit, who works when, and where, and how He pleases. So also are all other elect persons, who are incapable of being outwardly called by the ministry of the Word. . . . God did, from all eternity, decree to justify all the elect, and Christ did, in the fullness of time, die for their sins, and rise again for their justification: nevertheless, they are not justified until the Holy Spirit doth, in due time, actually apply Christ unto them" (*The Westminster Confession of Faith*, chapters 10.3 and 11.4).

Roman Catholic: "The Synod furthermore declares that . . . the beginning of the said Justification is to be derived from the prevenient grace of God, through Jesus Christ . . . that so they, who by sins were alienated from God, may be disposed through His quickening and assisting grace, to convert themselves to their own justification, by freely assenting to and cooperating with that said grace" (*Canons and Decrees of the Council of Trent*, Session 6, chapter 5).

Wesleyan/Methodist: "The condition of man after the fall of Adam is such that he cannot turn and prepare himself, by his own natural strength and works, to faith and calling upon God; wherefore we have not power to do good works, pleasant and acceptable to God, without the grace of God by Christ preventing us, that we may have a good will, and working with us, when we have that good will" (*Methodist Articles of Religion*, article 8).

Baptist: "We believe that the blessings of salvation are made free to all by the Gospel; that it is the immediate duty of all to accept them by a cordial, penitent, and obedient faith; and that nothing prevents the salvation of the greatest sinner on earth but his own inherent depravity and voluntary rejection of the Gospel; which rejection involves him in an aggravated condemnation" (*The New Hampshire Baptist Confession*, article 6).

Liberal: "Theologically, the content of Christology is to be found by asking two questions: 'From what do men need to be saved?' and 'How is Jesus related to man's salvation?' If the source of our sin is located in a non-psychological 'nature' which we inherit, we shall, of course, interpret the work of Christ in terms of His 'natures,' divine and human. But if we think of sin concretely and refer it to its psychological causes, we shall interpret salvation in terms of conscious experience. We shall then not ask concerning the 'nature' of Jesus, but rather concerning His religious consciousness and life. We shall emphasize His *God-consciousness* and His ability to create in His disciples a trust in God, which gives spiritual insight and moral power. As Schleiermacher declared, the important thing about Jesus is His God-consciousness" (Gerald Birney Smith in *A Guide to the Study of the Christian Religion*, pp. 531–32).

Point to Remember

I am not ashamed of the gospel, for it is the power of God for salvation to everyone who believes, to the Jew first and also to the Greek. Romans 1:16

To prepare for "Distinguishing Law and Gospel," read Galatians 3:21–24.

Distinguishing Law and Gospel

"We've learned to embrace what we are rather than hide it like an affliction."

—the mutant heroine Storm, from the film *X-Men*

In our society we hear a lot about discrimination. Employers, for example, announce that they do not discriminate on the basis of age, race, sex, or other criteria. Reputations can be ruined by the mere accusation of discrimination. But discriminating, which simply means "making distinctions," is often a useful—even necessary!—skill. Despite the negative connotations the word may have, we all discriminate. Under certain circumstances, it is even to be encouraged.

23. In what ways do you discriminate or make distinctions in your daily life? Think of circumstances under which discrimination may be necessary. Why is it so?

Handle With Care

24. Read 1 Timothy 1:8 and 2 Timothy 2:15. What instructions are given to Timothy about the use of God's Word?

25. Read 2 Corinthians 3:5–11. In this passage, what two things does Paul compare and contrast? What are the effects of each?

26. Read Galatians 3:15–25. In this passage, what two things does Paul compare and contrast? How are they related?

27. Compare Exodus 20:1–17 and Isaiah 53 with Romans 2:1–9 and Ephesians 1:2–8. What do such passages reveal about the location of Law and Gospel in Scripture?

28. Read Luke 4:16–21, followed by Acts 10:43. What do these passages say about the content of Scripture? How might this influence your understanding of Law and Gospel in the Old and New Testaments?

29. Compare 1 Timothy 1:15 and Romans 6:23. As Paul explains God's Word to his audiences, how does he summarize and emphasize its content?

30. Read Hebrews 11:6. How might this passage confirm the necessity of properly distinguishing between the Law and the Gospel?

Divine Discernment

Discrimination between different foods and medicines is not merely an intellectual exercise. It can be, in some situations, a matter of life and death. So it is with those desiring to be fed with and healed by God's holy Word.

31. In the light of passages read in the previous questions, why is it so vitally important that every Christian understand the difference between God's Word of Law and His Word of Gospel?

32. How may a proper understanding of the distinction between Law and Gospel affect the way in which you daily read and study the Bible?

Test Your Skills

We do hear a lot about discrimination. But perhaps not enough! St. Paul warns us that God's Word must be correctly handled; he informs us that the Law is good—but only if used properly. In humble thanksgiving for this precious gift of God's Word, the Christian responds with the desire to use this gift faithfully and properly, distinguishing carefully between Law and Gospel.

33. How might you respond to the oversimplified comment that the Old Testament contains the Law while the New Testament contains the Gospel?

Comparisons

Dividing participants into small groups, look up the following Bible passages. Which contain Law? Which contain Gospel? Do some passages contain both? Neither? Mark your answer in the appropriate box, and share your results with the larger group.

Scripture	Law	Gospel	Both	Other
Exodus 20:3				
John 3:16				
Ephesians 2:8–10				
Leviticus 11:7–8				
Mark 16:16				
Job 19:25–27				
Luke 22:19–20				
1 Timothy 5:23				
Isaiah 9:6–7				
Hebrews 13:1				
Colossians 3:1–4				

Point to Remember

The letter kills, but the Spirit gives life. 2 Corinthians 3:6

To prepare for "Applying Law and Gospel," read Romans 3:20–26.

Applying Law and Gospel

Careless talk costs lives.

—World War II security slogan

In the context of war, saying the wrong thing to the wrong person at the wrong time can be a deadly mistake. But even off the battlefield, our words can have serious and unintentional consequences if we do not choose and speak them carefully. Sometimes we say too much, sometimes too little. Sometimes we say the wrong thing; sometimes we speak at the wrong time.

34. Think of a time when your words had results that were unintended. What was the cause of these unexpected results? What could you have said or done differently?

Completing the Task

35. Read Acts 20:24 and Romans 10:16–17. How does Paul describe his task as a preacher? Why is his task a necessary one?

36. Read Matthew 5:17–20 and Psalm 19:12. Why is it necessary that God's servants faithfully proclaim the Law as well as the Gospel?

37. Compare the sermons recorded in Acts 2:22–39 and Acts 3:13–26. How does Peter apply both Law and Gospel to his hearers? In what order are they proclaimed? Why?

38. Compare Matthew 19:16–26 and Acts 16:25–33. What answers are given to the question asked in these passages? What may account for the different responses given?

39. Read Galatians 3:26–29 and Titus 3:4–7. What is related to the Gospel in these passages? How is it related?

40. Read Matthew 26:26–28. What is related to the Gospel in these passages? How is it related?

41. Read Ephesians 5:25–27. Compare John 8:31–32 and Romans 16:17. How do these passages describe the relationship between the Gospel and the church?

Aptly Applied

God's Word is powerful. His Word of Law and His Word of Gospel, however, each produce very different results. For this reason it is important that each is applied properly, at the right time, in the right amount, and in the right order.

42. Considering the above, what comfort do you take in knowing that God Himself has appointed and ordained ministers of Word and Sacrament?

43. Christians not only hear Law and Gospel proclaimed by their pastor; they also communicate each in conversation with friends and neighbors. In the light of questions 36 and 37, what important considerations will affect an individual's application of Law and Gospel? Why?

A Faith-Filled Response

Our God is a gracious God. Not only has He revealed Himself in Scripture; He has appointed pastors to proclaim His Word faithfully. Through them He applies His Gospel not only by means of the spoken Word, but also through the means of Baptism and Holy Communion. A gracious God indeed!

44. How might you respond to a Christian friend who believes that regular worship attendance is unnecessary? How might you explain the benefits of frequent worship?

45. As part of your devotions this week, read Martin Luther's "Christian Questions with Their Answers" (*Lutheran Worship*, pp. 306–7). How do these questions apply Law and Gospel to those preparing to receive Communion?

Comparisons

Eastern Orthodox: "What must we join with prayer in order to be grounded in the hope of salvation and blessedness? Our own exertions for the attainment of blessedness (Luke 6:46; Matthew 7:21). What doctrine may we take as our guide in these exertions? The doctrine of our Lord Jesus Christ, which is briefly set forth in His Beatitudes, or sentences on blessedness" (*The Longer Catechism of the Eastern Church*, questions 435–36).

Lutheran: "We believe, teach, and confess that the distinction between the Law and the Gospel is to be maintained in the Church with great diligence as an especially brilliant light, by which, according to the admonition of St. Paul, the Word of God is rightly divided" (Epitome of the Formula of Concord V 1).

Reformed/Presbyterian: "They whom God has accepted in His Beloved, effectually called and sanctified by His Spirit, can neither totally nor finally fall away from the state of grace; but shall certainly persevere therein to the end, and be eternally saved. . . . Nevertheless they may . . . fall into grievous sins; and for a time continue therein; whereby they incur God's displeasure, and grieve His Holy Spirit; come to be deprived of some measure of their graces and comforts; have their hearts hardened, and their consciences wounded; hurt and scandalize others, and bring temporal judgments upon themselves" (*The Westminster Confession of Faith*, chapter 17.1, 3).

Roman Catholic: "If anyone says, that the man who is justified and howsoever perfect, is not bound to observe the commandments of God and of the Church, but only to believe; as if indeed the Gospel were a bare and absolute promise of eternal life, without the condition of observing the commandments; let him be anathema. If anyone says, that Jesus Christ was given by God to men as a Redeemer in whom to trust, and not also as a Legislator whom to obey; let him be anathema." (*Canons and Decrees of the Council of Trent*, Session 6, On Justification, canons 20–21).

Baptist: "We believe that the Law of God is the eternal and unchangeable rule of His moral government; that it is holy, just, and good; and that the inability which the Scriptures ascribe to fallen men to fulfill its precepts arises entirely from their love of sin; to deliver them from which, and to restore them through a Mediator to unfeigned obedience to the holy Law, is one great end of the Gospel, and of the means of grace connected with the establishment of the visible Church" (*The New Hampshire Baptist Confession*, article 12).

Wesleyan/Methodist: "Original sin stands not in the following of Adam (as the Pelagians do vainly talk), but it is the corruption of the nature of every man, that naturally is engendered of the offspring of Adam, whereby man is very far gone from original righteousness, and of his own nature inclined to evil, and that continually" (*Methodist Articles of Religion*, article 7).

Liberal: "Today we are coming more and more to think of religion as a normal and natural experience. Those who confuse experience with its doctrinal interpretation are greatly perplexed by this tendency, for it seems like abandoning fundamental realities of Christianity. But the history of religion has made us aware that, so far as the supernaturalistic details of a doctrine of salvation are concerned, these appear in various forms in pagan religions as well as in Christianity. . . . The distinctive qualities of Christian salvation must be looked for in the kind of moral and religious character produced by Christian faith" (Gerald Birney Smith in *A Guide to the Study of the Christian Religion*, p. 523).

Point to Remember

But I do not account my life of any value nor as precious to myself, if only I may finish my course and the ministry that I received from the Lord Jesus, to testify to the gospel of the grace of God. Acts 20:24

To prepare for "Law, Gospel, and Justification," read Ephesians 2:1–9.

Law, Gospel, and Justification

Though justice be thy plea, consider this,
That in the course of justice none of us
Should see salvation.

—Portia in Shakespeare's *The Merchant of Venice*

"I was perfectly justified!" Such is often the cry of those seeking to escape punishment. The claim—in the courtroom as well as in popular use—is a legal claim, an appeal to the laws of the state or to commonly accepted ideas of right and wrong. A lawyer, for example, may argue that his client committed no murder; rather, it was "justifiable homicide." That is, it was legal homicide, an act not condemned by the law.

46. Think of a time when you may have argued that your actions were "perfectly justified." On what basis did you believe this to be the case? Was it in fact true?

Just an Observation

47. Compare Galatians 2:15–16 and Galatians 5:4. What is the Law incapable of doing? Why can it not do this?

48. Read Galatians 3:21–24. How does Paul refer to the Law in this passage? What is its relationship to the Gospel promise? What role does it play in preparing the way for salvation?

49. Compare Galatians 4:4–5 and Galatians 3:13. How do these passages describe the relationship between Jesus and the Law?

50. Compare Colossians 2:13–14 and Romans 10:4. How does Christ's relationship to the Law affect the Christian's relationship to the Law?

51. Compare Romans 16:25–27 and 1 Corinthians 15:1–4. How do these passages describe the relationship between Jesus and the Gospel?

52. Read Colossians 1:21–23. What are the effects of the Gospel? What relationship does Paul urge Christians to maintain with the Gospel?

Sons and Heirs

Thanks be to God, we have no need of appealing to the Law. Thanks be to God, we have been redeemed from the Law! Jesus Himself suffered what we lawfully deserved, giving us instead a free and unearned pardon.

53. As you consider Jesus' relationship with the Law, what comfort can you take in the circumstances of His birth, life, and death?

54. In the light of question 52, what means are available to assist you to "continue in the faith, stable and steadfast" (Colossians 1:23)? Why is it particularly important that the Christian make use of these means?

All about Christ

The Christian can indeed proclaim, "I was perfectly justified!" This claim can be made confidently even in the court of God Himself. But it is not made with an appeal to the Law. The Christian instead appeals to Christ, whose perfect life and perfect death are the basis for our perfect justification.

55. How might you respond to a friend who believes that both believing the Gospel and obeying the Law are necessary for salvation? In simple language, how might you clarify the distinctive purposes of Law and Gospel?

Comparisons

Church Body	Original Sin	Law's Purpose	Gospel's Purpose	Salvation
Eastern Orthodox	Stained soul; will able to cooperate with grace.	Show God's will for our lives.	Provide empowering grace, yielding obedience.	Ultimately depends on the Christian's obedience.
Lutheran	Thoroughly corrupted soul; will turned completely against God.	Point out our sin, restrain evil, and show God's will for our lives.	Provide forgiving grace through Word and Sacrament.	Assured to all who believe in Christ's perfect obedience and sacrifice.
Reformed/ Presbyterian	Thoroughly corrupted soul; will turned completely against God.	Point out our sin, restrain evil, and show God's will for our lives.	Provide forgiving grace, symbolized by Word and Sacrament.	Never sure, as it is given only to the elect, those whom God has pre-chosen.
Roman Catholic	Corrupted soul; will able to cooperate with grace.	Show God's will for our lives.	Provide empowering grace, yielding obedience.	Ultimately depends on the Christian's obedience.
Baptist	Thoroughly corrupted soul; will greatly impaired.	Show God's will for our lives.	Provide grace so that will chooses salvation.	Ultimately depends on the Christian's decision.
Wesleyan/ Methodist	Thoroughly corrupted soul; will greatly impaired.	Show God's will for our lives.	Provide grace so that will chooses salvation.	Ultimately depends on the Christian's decision.
Liberal	Primarily a psychological experience.	Man-made for life in community.	Model of Jesus' ethical life.	Pertains only to betterment of this life.

Point to Remember

For by grace you have been saved through faith. And this is not your own doing; it is the gift of God, not a result of works, so that no one may boast. Ephesians 2:8–9

To prepare for "Law, Gospel, and Sanctification," read Ephesians 2:10.

Law, Gospel, and Sanctification

Is that which is holy loved by the gods because it is holy,
or is it holy because it is loved by the gods?

—Plato

Even the pagan philosopher Plato was greatly concerned with the issue of holiness. In our modern society, however, *holy* has become a four-letter word in more than the literal sense. Though we are inundated with aids and advice for self-help and self-improvement, holiness, it seems, is not something to which our world aspires. To the contrary, being "holier than thou" is an accusation with which no one wants to be charged.

56. Why do you suppose many people have such an aversion to talking about holiness? With what do you think most people outside of the Christian church associate the word *holy*?

A Faith That Works

57. Compare James 2:26 and Ephesians 2:8–10. What do these passages have to say about the relationship between Law and Gospel in the Christian's life?

58. Read Romans 6:14–18. How does Paul's explanation further clarify your answer to question 57?

59. Compare Matthew 15:1–9 and 1 Timothy 4:1–3. What distinction is made between works that are truly good and other forms of obedience? On what basis is this distinction made?

60. In the first session of this study two uses of the Law were discussed. Read Psalm 119:9–16 and Psalm 119:105–6. In what further manner does the psalmist say the Law is to be used?

61. Compare Colossians 3:8–10 and 1 Peter 2:5. What illustrations do the authors use? Who is at work in the continual process being illustrated?

62. Compare John 17:17–19; Philippians 1:4–6; and Philippians 2:12–13. How do these passages further clarify your answer to question 59?

63. Compare Romans 7:18–23 and Philippians 3:12–14. What does Paul's own experience tell us about the nature of sanctification?

64. Compare Galatians 3:1–5 and Galatians 6:13–14. What strong warning does Paul give about misunderstanding sanctification?

Saint and Sinner

Holiness is by no means something to be avoided, neither in conversation nor in life. It is commanded by our holy God Himself. And yet, as we must confess, we are incapable of making ourselves holy.

65. What consolation can you take in knowing that sanctification is not left to your own power?

66. As you consider your own sanctification, what comfort do you take in knowing that even the great St. Paul continually struggled with sin?

Christ in Action

"Holy, holy, holy" the church sings in the Sanctus. It is a description of our God, but it also describes God's desire for His people. He so desires our holiness that He not only declares us holy for the sake of His Son, Jesus Christ, but also, through the working of His Holy Spirit, He Himself acts to make us holy.

67. How might you respond to the popular misconception that "God is responsible for our justification, but we are responsible for our sanctification"?

68. How might you respond to a friend who believes that, since Christ fulfilled the Law, Christians have no need of hearing the Law preached?

Comparisons

Progressive Sanctification: Some church bodies today teach that sanctification, God's process whereby He effectively makes us holy, is progressive. The Lutheran church teaches that sanctification may vary at different times in a person's life (Romans 7:14–19; Galatians 2:11; 5:17; 1 John 1:8).

Possibility of Sanctification: Lutheran Christians, along with Presbyterians and some Evangelicals, teach that perfect sanctification in this life, due to the persistent effects of the devil, the world, and our sinful flesh, is impossible, and that Christians claiming to be sinless have, under the influence of Satan, deceived themselves (1 John 1:8, 10; John 8:44). Other church bodies, particularly the Eastern Orthodox and Roman Catholic churches, teach that perfect sanctification is difficult to obtain, but it can be done—the saints, for example. Still others, particularly from the Wesleyan family of church bodies, including the Methodists, Pentecostals, and Holiness groups, teach that perfect sanctification is attainable in this life by any Christian earnestly seeking it.

Requirement of Sanctification: Correlative with their doctrine of purgatory, the Roman Catholic Church insists that perfect sanctification is required before enjoying the beatific vision of God. Upon death, the saints, due to their achievement of perfect holiness, enter immediately into heaven. Those not achieving full sanctification in this life are "purged" (hence, "purgatory") of their sins after death for an indeterminate time until they are able to enter God's presence.

Point to Remember

We were buried therefore with Him by baptism into death. Romans 6:4

Leader Guide

This guide is provided as a "safety net," a place to turn for help in answering questions and for enriching discussion. It will not answer every question raised in your class. Please read it, along with the questions, before class. Consult it in class only after exploring the Bible references and discussing what they teach. Please note the different abilities of your class members. Some will easily find the Bible passages listed in this study; others will struggle. To make participation easier, team up members of the class. For example, if a question asks you to look up several passages, assign one passage to one group, the second to another, and so on. Divide the work! Let participants present the answers they discover.

Each topic is divided into four easy-to-use sections.

Focus introduces key concepts that will be discovered.

Inform guides the participants into Scripture to uncover truths concerning a doctrine.

Connect enables participants to apply what is learned in Scripture to their lives and provides them an opportunity to formulate and articulate a defense of a key doctrine.

Vision provides participants with practical suggestions for extending the theme of the lesson out of the classroom and into the world.

Also take note of the Comparisons section at the end of each lesson. The editor has drawn this material from the official confessional documents and historical works of the various denominations. The passages describe and compare the denominations so that students can see how Lutherans differ from other Christians and also see how all Christians share many of the same beliefs and practices. The passages are not polemical.

God's Word: The Law

Objectives

By the power of the Holy Spirit working through God's Word, participants will (1) understand the nature of God's Law, (2) recognize the purpose for which God's Law has been given, and (3) appreciate the rich blessings of Christ, who has fulfilled the Law in our place.

Opening Worship

It may prove beneficial to begin this study of God's Law with a reading of God's Law. The Ten Commandments may be read in Exodus 20:1–17, or, if time allows, the Commandments with Luther's explanations may be read from the Small Catechism. The hymn "The Law of God Is Good and Wise" (*Lutheran Worship* 329) is particularly suited to the emphases of this session. Selected verses from Psalm 119, a meditation on God's Law, might also be read as an appropriate prayer.

Focus

1. Read, or ask a participant to read, the first paragraph. Spend some time discussing the reasons for feeling that certain laws are inconvenient. It will likely be evident that the reason most of us dislike certain laws is simply that they prevent us from doing what we want to do. This is precisely their goal! Emphasize that God, knowing all too well our sinful nature, has lovingly given us His divine Law to prevent us from succumbing to sin and being driven even further from Him.

Holy Legality (Inform)

God's Law, like God Himself, is holy, righteous, and good. Though it threatens and accuses sinners, the Law does so as part of God's plan to reveal our sin and our consequent need for salvation. He Himself has mercifully provided this salvation in the person of Christ, who both fulfilled the Law and suffered its condemnation on our behalf.

2. Exhorting the Christians of Ephesus to live a holy and God-pleasing life, St. Paul distinguishes between those who are wise and unwise. The wise, he explains, are those who "understand what the will of the Lord is." The psalmist, clearly one of the wise, proclaims that he earnestly desires to do the will of God. He goes on to say that he knows God's will because he knows God's Law. The Law of God does indeed express His will for our life. For this reason, the Lutheran Confessions can refer to the Law quite simply as "the immutable will of God" (Ep VI 7). Not only does the Law teach "what is right and pleasing to God," but it also "reproves everything that is sin and contrary to God's will" (Ep V 3). Because the Law expresses nothing less than the will of a holy, righteous, and good God, Paul can also explain that the Law itself is "holy and righteous and good."

3. Because the Law expresses God's holy and perfect will for His creation, He desires that all clearly know what this will is. To this end He gave the written Law to His Old Testament people. The summary of God's Law, the Ten Commandments, Moses received on two stone tablets. Not all are descended from Israel, however. Not all have been taught the Ten Commandments as Israel was commanded to teach her children. Are some then without the Law? This is the question Paul answers in the opening chapters of Romans. While admitting that the Gentiles "do not have the law"—that is, the written Law given to Israel—he explains that "they show that the work of the law is written on their hearts." In fact, this "natural" law was given to all people even before the "revealed" Law of the Commandments. Thus the confessors write that those before Moses (even those before the fall into sin) "had the Law of God written also into their hearts, because they were created in the image of God" (Ep VI 2). To be sure, sinful human nature prevents a perfect understanding of this natural law; but it does not prevent all understanding. For this reason Paul can explain that the Gentiles are without excuse, because, as the reformers wrote, "Man's reason or natural intellect indeed has still a dim spark of the knowledge that there is a God, as also of the doctrine of the Law" (SD II 9).

4. While Scripture is clear that all know the Law, it is also perfectly clear that none keep the Law. The author of Ecclesiastes announces that there is no one "who does good and never sins" (Ecclesiastes 7:20). John goes on to explain the relationship between sin and the Law, stating that "everyone who makes a practice of

41

sinning also practices lawlessness; sin is lawlessness" (1 John 3:4). In agreement with St. John, the Lutheran Confessions bluntly state, "Sin is everything that is contrary to God's Law" (SD VI 14). Lest people be tempted to think lightly of sin, to downplay their own sinfulness by believing they keep *most* of the Law, sinning only occasionally or breaking only minor points of the Law, James takes pains to explain the folly of this thinking. With a sweeping condemnation he declares that "whoever keeps the whole law but fails in one point has become accountable for all of it" (2:10). In this light, it is perfectly understandable that the confessors would note that "all Scripture, all the church cries out that the Law cannot be satisfied" (Ap III 45).

5. The Law of God is not static. God Himself uses it to produce certain effects. In fact, the Law can be put to several uses. (Note: The Lutheran Confessions denote three uses of the Law [see Ep VI 1]. Two of these apply to all people, while the third applies only to those who have first been called and redeemed by the Gospel. Discussion of this third use will therefore be reserved for a later session: "Law, Gospel, and Sanctification.") Timothy, while noting that care must be taken to use the Law properly, gives some indication of one of its uses. He says it was made "for the lawless and disobedient, for the ungodly and sinners, for the unholy and profane" (1 Timothy 1:9). The Law and its threat of punishment are to prevent these people from doing what their sinful nature would otherwise compel them to do. This is referred to as the first use of the Law. Luther states in the Confessions: "We hold that the Law was given by God, first, to restrain sin by threats and the dread of punishment" (SA-III II 1). Likewise, the confessors note that the Law was given "first, that thereby outward discipline might be maintained against wild, disobedient men" (Ep VI 1).

6. The Law is meant not only to prevent sin; it also reveals sin. Paul says that it is *only* through the Law that sin is revealed. He confesses, "If it had not been for the law, I would not have known sin" (Romans 7:7). Paul does not merely comment on his own experience; expressing the same thought elsewhere, he notes that "through the law comes knowledge of sin" (Romans 3:20). Because it is only by means of the Law that we become conscious of sin, this second use of the Law is what the Confessions call its chief use: "the chief office or force of the Law is that it reveal original sin with all its fruits, and show man how very low his nature has fallen" (SA-III II 4).

7. In addition to revealing man's sin, the second use of the Law also reveals the consequences of sin. It reveals that the holy and sinless

God—who also created His people to be holy and sinless—does not at all take sin lightly. He Himself announces, "Cursed be anyone who does not confirm the words of this law by doing them" (Deuteronomy 27:26). The ultimate consequence of this curse, Paul explains, is death, both temporal and eternal. It is in the light of such scriptural testimony that the authors of the Lutheran Confessions acknowledge that the Law "threatens its transgressors with God's wrath and temporal and eternal punishments" (SD V 17). Even more strongly, they write that we are "accused or condemned by God's Law, so that we are by nature the children of wrath, death, and damnation, unless we are delivered therefrom by the merit of Christ" (SD I 6).

8. Though the Law has different uses, there is one thing for which it is not to be used. St Paul, a former proponent of the Law, makes this point again and again in his letters to the early Christian churches. "Now it is evident that no one is justified before God by the law" (Galatians 3:11), he writes. He goes even further, stating bluntly that "you are severed from Christ, you who would be justified by the law" (Galatians 5:4). This is obviously no small point. Though the Law expresses God's will; though it is holy, righteous, and good; and though it has many uses, it cannot effect salvation. Paul goes so far as to say that those who try to use it for this end have instead forfeited salvation. The confessors could therefore reach no conclusion other than that "it is evident that we are not justified by the Law. Otherwise, why would there be need of Christ or the Gospel?" (Ap III 136).

Crime and Punishment (Connect)

9. It is impossible to be nonchalant when meditating on the Law of God. It not only commands and prohibits; it points out our failure to obey and the dire consequences that result. If your meditation on the Law produces "true terrors, contrition, and sorrow" then you have properly understood it (SD II 54; see SA-III II 4). It is time to hear the Gospel!

10. Paul had reminded his readers of God's Old Testament announcement of a curse on all those who do not fulfill the Law. He also reminds them of another biblical curse: "Cursed is everyone who is hanged on a tree" (Galatians 3:13). This, says Paul, applies even to Jesus Himself who hung on the cross. But how could the sinless Christ who fulfilled the Law be cursed? Paul explains that He became "a curse for us," in our place. He who fulfilled the Law received the

punishment deserved by those who have not. Thanks be to God! Those condemned by the Law have been redeemed from the curse of the Law.

Utter Silence (Vision)

11. Many do not know the Ten Commandments. Others may know them and reject them. Yet all people recognize and live their lives according to some form of law, some understanding of right and wrong. Conversation with unbelievers might begin with an attempt to understand the nature of the "law" they follow. On the basis of their explanation, you might emphasize the common ground between what they believe, what all people believe, and what is stated in the Commandments. It might then be pointed out that these commonalities suggest a common source—God Himself. Furthermore, you might ask what happens when they do not fulfill their own "law." What consequences result? You could point out that the inability to keep even those laws which we acknowledge is an indication that there is something fundamentally wrong with mankind. Our inability to keep the Law reveals our need for the Gospel.

God's Word: The Gospel

Objectives

By the power of the Holy Spirit working through God's Word, participants will (1) understand the peculiar nature of the Gospel and the manner in which it differs from the Law, (2) recognize and be able to articulate the specific content of the Gospel message, and (3) appreciate and give thanks for the free forgiveness of sins which the Gospel communicates.

Opening Worship

Opening worship might begin with a responsive reading of the Second Article of the Creed and Luther's explanation in the Small Catechism, which particularly highlights the Gospel's content and power. The same is true of "The Gospel Shows the Father's Grace" (*Lutheran Worship* 330), which may be sung together. As the Gospel is the good news by which the church is called into existence, an appropriate prayer may be For the Church (*Lutheran Worship*, p. 124).

Focus

12. Read, or ask a participant to read, the first paragraph. Spend some time discussing recent events in the news. Encourage participants to share the last piece of good news they heard. This may be simple for some. It may be more difficult, however, to recall some good news that had immediate and personal relevance. By way of contrast, emphasize that although the death and resurrection of Christ is "old news"—2,000 years old—it remains the best news. No matter how many times this news is heard, it never loses its personal relevance.

Power Points (Inform)

The Christian faith and life are set on the foundation of the Gospel of Jesus Christ. This Gospel is the central doctrine of Christian theology, that which distinguishes the Christian faith from all other religions and philosophies. It is, in short, the peculiar good news of Christ's death and resurrection for the free forgiveness of sins.

13. In this brief, memorable definition of the Gospel, St. Paul refers to it as "the power of God for salvation to everyone who believes" (Romans 1:16). Even in such a short phrase he manages to highlight the manner in which the Gospel differs from the Law. Two differences can be here noted. First, the Gospel is not about doing what is commanded; it is about believing what is promised. And most important, unlike the Law, which cannot justify, Paul specifically states that the Gospel is "for salvation." These significant differences are concisely expressed in the Apology of the Augsburg Confession: "The Gospel, which is properly the promise of the remission of sins and of justification for Christ's sake, proclaims the righteousness of faith in Christ, which the Law does not teach" (Ap IV 43).

14. The apostle Paul requests the prayers of the Ephesians so that his proclamation of the Gospel may be made clearly and boldly. Significantly, he refers to the Gospel as a "mystery." Unlike the Law, which is written on the hearts of all men, the Gospel cannot be known by natural human reason. In this light, Paul's request is quite urgent; unless the Gospel which has been revealed *to* him is subsequently revealed *by* him in his preaching, men will remain in their sins. What is more, because reason cannot comprehend it, the Gospel will not be believed unless this belief is effected by God Himself. This is indicated when Paul notes that unbelievers are "blinded" and are kept "from seeing the light of the gospel" (2 Corinthians 4:4). For this reason, while noting that man's mind has some knowledge of the Law, the Lutheran Confessions go on to explain that "it is so ignorant, blind, and perverted that when even the most ingenious and learned men upon the earth read or hear the Gospel of the Son of God and the promise of eternal salvation, they cannot from their own powers perceive, apprehend, understand, or believe and regard it as true" (SD II 9).

15. Timothy, who is himself a young preacher of the Gospel, is told that Christ "gave Himself as a ransom for all" (1 Timothy 2:6) because He "desires all people to be saved" (1 Timothy 2:4). This bit of information is particularly relevant for those appointed to the task of proclaiming God's Word. Christ did not die only for some; nor is God stingy with His Good News. Christ's death covered the sins of all men; He therefore desires His Gospel of forgiveness to be preached to all men. The apostle Peter very much agrees with Paul, assuring his readers that God is "not wishing that any should perish" (2 Peter 3:9).

In agreement with both Peter and Paul, the Formula of Concord insists that "Christ calls to Himself all sinners and promises them rest, and He is in earnest that all men should come to Him" (Ep XI 8). Likewise, it rejects the notion that "God is unwilling that every one should be saved, but that some, without regard to their sins, from the mere counsel, purpose, and will of God, are ordained to condemnation so that they cannot be saved" (Ep XI 19).

16. Mark begins his life of the Savior by calling it "the gospel of Jesus Christ" (1:1). Paul, writing to the Corinthian church, mentions that he has preached "the gospel of Christ" (2 Corinthians 2:12). In the same manner, when he refers to the Gospel in his Letter to the Romans, he calls it "the ministry of the gospel of Christ" (15:19). As most Christians have learned, the word *Gospel* simply and literally means "Good News." But the apostles and evangelists do not have just any good news to share; it is very specific news. It is the Good News about Christ, it is His Gospel. Thus the reformers state that "the Gospel presents to us Christ" (Ap XII 76) and further clarify that "the Gospel is such a preaching as shows and gives nothing else than grace and forgiveness in Christ" (SD V 12). No matter how good the news, if it is not about Jesus, it is not the Gospel of the Scripture. As its authors emphasize time and again, Jesus stands at the beginning, center, and end of the Christian Gospel.

17. In the early days of the church, as in our own day, there were those who not only misunderstood the Gospel but who also misapplied it. In an attempt to prevent this, Paul writes to the Corinthians, reminding them of the Gospel as he had purely preached it. In doing so, he highlights three important events: Christ's death for our sins, His burial, and His resurrection on the third day. Even more succinctly, he had reminded them earlier that when he was with them he endeavored to preach nothing "except Jesus Christ and Him crucified" (1 Corinthians 2:2). Christ's death and resurrection is the only basis on which the forgiveness of sins and eternal life rests. As such, it is the only basis on which the Gospel can be proclaimed. Christ's death and resurrection for our salvation *is* the Gospel. As the Lutheran Confessions state, "This is the very voice peculiar to the Gospel, namely, that for Christ's sake, and not for the sake of our works, we obtain by faith remission of sins" (Ap III 153).

18. Not only do the writings of Paul purely set forth the Gospel message; they also offer strong warnings against being deceived by false gospels and those who preach them. The apostle harshly rebukes

the Galatians for "turning to a different gospel—not that there is another one" (1:6–7). But he saves his strongest words for those who were guilty of misleading them, those trying to "distort the gospel of Christ" (1:7). With righteous anger Paul prays that such men be eternally condemned. Though it may sound extreme, Paul's reaction is by no means an overreaction. He is well aware of what is at stake. The context of his letter makes clear that some in Galatia were preaching works as if they were necessary for salvation. No, says Paul; to mingle Law and Gospel is to pervert the Gospel and thereby endanger salvation. This confusion of Law and Gospel is something with which not only Paul had to deal; it was also very much at the heart of the debates of the Reformation. The reformers, therefore, had to clarify that "the Gospel is not a preaching of repentance or reproof, but properly nothing else than a preaching of consolation, and a joyful message which does not reprove or terrify, but comforts consciences against the terrors of the Law, points alone to the merits of Christ, and raises them up again by the lovely preaching of the grace and favor of God, obtained through Christ's merit" (Ep V 7).

Living by Faith (Connect)

19. As Paul notes, the Gospel is a mystery; it is not self-evident. Furthermore, because of our sinful nature, we may misunderstand or even be tempted to reject the Gospel after having received it. But God Himself stirs up and strengthens our faith. This faith, Paul writes, comes by hearing the Word of the Gospel itself (Romans 10:17). For this reason Christians eagerly take advantage of opportunities to have their forgiveness announced and their faith strengthened where and when the Good News is preached.

20. It is easy to be swept along by the tide of popular preaching and writing that portrays Christianity in a light not dissimilar to many self-help groups. But the Gospel, properly speaking, is like no other teaching. By frequent study of God's Word and sound Christian doctrine we become equipped not only to recognize the Gospel and to distinguish it from contrary messages, but also to refute false teachings that may otherwise endanger our faith and salvation.

Communicating the Message (Vision)

21. Although it may seem strange to us, there are indeed many who find the Gospel too good to be true. *Free* forgiveness, they say; I don't have to do *anything*? There is, however, nothing that is too good to be true. Truth is not a matter of good or bad; quite simply, something is either true or it is not. The New Testament authors go to great lengths to verify the truth of the news they preach. Explaining the Gospel to the Corinthians, Paul specifically mentions that the resurrected Christ had been seen by hundreds of people, most of whom were still alive to be consulted (1 Corinthians 15:1–8). The news of Jesus' death and resurrection is indeed true; happily, this true news is also good news.

22. The Galatian church is not unique in its misguided attempts to turn the Gospel into the Law. This happens even today when Jesus is emphasized as a moral example or new lawgiver rather than as the One who both fulfilled the Law and suffered its consequences in our stead. To be sure, the sinless life of Jesus does provide a perfect moral example! And Scripture does encourage us to imitate this example (see Philippians 2:5). As we are all too aware, however, a perfect example is an example to which we cannot live up. Our gross lack of perfection is, in fact, what prompted Christ's incarnation, death, and resurrection—not merely to provide us with an example, but to redeem us. This redemption through Christ is the very Gospel itself.

Distinguishing Law and Gospel

Objectives

By the power of the Holy Spirit working through God's Word, participants will (1) understand the proper biblical distinction between Law and Gospel, (2) recognize the practical importance of properly distinguishing between the two, and (3) appreciate the divine purposes for which God has revealed both Law and Gospel to His people.

Opening Worship

If participants are willing, and if time allows, the brief service of Individual Confession and Absolution (*Lutheran Worship*, pp. 310–11) may be recited to highlight the difference between the work of the Law and that of the Gospel. The hymn "God's Word Is Our Great Heritage" (*Lutheran Worship* 333) may be sung or simply read together as a prayer of thanksgiving for God's Word of Law and Gospel.

Focus

23. Read, or ask a participant to read, the first paragraph. Spend some time discussing the ways in which the word *discrimination* is popularly used, both positively and negatively. Encourage participants to offer examples of everyday distinctions they themselves make. Highlight those examples in which discrimination seems especially necessary and encourage participants to articulate the reasons for its necessity. Building on this, the great importance of distinguishing between God's Law and His Gospel can be emphasized.

Handle with Care (Inform)

Having in the previous sessions discussed the natures and uses of both Law and Gospel, it becomes important to further clarify their proper distinction. This distinction is not arbitrary or invented; it is revealed in Scripture itself as the means by which all of God's Word is to be rightly understood and interpreted. Properly understanding God's

Word, the Christian will properly understand God's will for his or her salvation.

24. Being appointed a preacher of Law and Gospel, Timothy is reminded that the Law is good—"if one uses it lawfully" (1 Timothy 1:8). He is to know that the Law can be used improperly and with harmful results. In the same manner, Paul exhorts Timothy to be one who is "rightly handling" (2 Timothy 2:15) the Word of God. Again, an incorrect use of God's Word may confuse and even lead astray those who hear its proclamation. Paul's advice is good pastoral advice. Knowing the power and effects of both the Law and the Gospel, Paul is concerned that Timothy rightly divide and properly proclaim each, neither confusing nor mingling them together. Paul's concern is highlighted in the Lutheran Confessions, which observe that if Law and Gospel are "mingled with one another" then "the merit of Christ is obscured and troubled consciences are robbed of their comfort" (SD V 1). Therefore the confessors also state, "We believe, teach, and confess that the distinction between the Law and the Gospel is to be maintained in the Church with great diligence as an especially bright light, by which, according to the admonition of St. Paul, the Word of God is rightly divided" (Ep V 2).

25. In his second Epistle to the Corinthians, Paul makes a clear distinction between what he calls "the letter" and "the Spirit" (3:6). He gives his readers a clue regarding the nature of the former by indicating that it came with letters engraved on stones, a reference to the two tables of the Law given to Moses. In verse 17 he further explains that the Lord Himself is the Spirit. The letter came with Moses, the Spirit with Christ. But Paul not only distinguishes between their names and origins; he also notes their radically different effects. He tells the Corinthians that "the letter kills, but the Spirit gives life" (3:6). This is certainly true. As noted in the first session, the chief use of the Law accuses us, condemns us, and announces the deadly consequences of our failure to obey God's commands. But, as noted in the second session, the proper function of the Gospel is to reveal Christ and the eternal life that he has won for us. The distinctly different effects of the Law and of the Gospel are also noted in the confessional writings of the Lutheran church. They confess that "whenever the Law alone, without the Gospel being added exercises this its office there is death and hell" (SA-III III 7). But when the Gospel is revealed—whether in Word or Sacrament—"it works forgiveness of sin, delivers from death and the devil, and gives eternal salvation" (SC IV 6).

51

26. When he writes to the Galatians, Paul also makes a distinction between two things found in Scripture. He here refers to them as the Law and the promises. As he explains their differences, he notes that the Law was "added because of transgressions" (3:19) and that it cannot impart life. By way of contrast, he notes that the Christian's inheritance "comes by promise" (3:18) so that this promise "might be given to those who believe" (3:22) This promise is clearly the Gospel promise of salvation, a promise received by Abraham in the Old Testament and later fulfilled with Christ's coming in the New Testament. Paul's distinction is maintained by the Lutheran confessors, who note that "all Scripture ought to be distributed into these two principal topics, the Law and the promises" (Ap IV 5). The Law and the promises, though different, are certainly not unrelated. Paul strongly insists that the Law is not opposed to the promises of God. Rather, he says, "The law was our guardian until Christ came" (Galatians 3:24). The authors of the Formula of Concord explain how the Law prepares sinners for and leads them to Christ and His Gospel: "Through the preaching of the Law and its threats in the ministry of the New Testament the hearts of impenitent men may be terrified, and brought to a knowledge of their sins and to repentance; but not in such a way that they lose heart and despair in this process, but that . . . they be comforted and strengthened again by the preaching of the holy Gospel concerning Christ" (SD V 24–25).

27. It is not infrequently heard that the Old Testament is Law while the New Testament is Gospel. This is understandable. The first four books of the New Testament are referred to as the Gospels; likewise, many New Testament figures (including Jesus Himself) use the word *Law* as a sort of shorthand in reference to either the books of Moses or the entire Old Testament. Yet, as these various passages make clear, the New Testament is not without the Law; nor is the Old Testament without the Gospel (see also previous answer). The confessors, especially eager to highlight the Gospel's Old Testament presence, make note of this when they write that "in some places it presents the Law, and in others the promise concerning Christ, namely, either when it promises that Christ will come [i.e., in the Old Testament], and offers, for His sake, the remission of sins, justification, and life eternal, or when, in the Gospel, Christ Himself, since He has appeared, promises the remission of sins, justification, and life eternal" (Ap IV 5).

28. Jesus shocked His audience in Nazareth. Reading from the prophet Isaiah, He concluded by announcing that Isaiah's Gospel promise was being fulfilled in their very presence. In terms unmistakable to His hearers, He announced that He was the Anointed One (i.e., the Messiah, the Christ) mentioned by the prophet. He was the One with whom the Good News arrived. This announcement was not lost on Jesus' disciples. Peter, in the Book of Acts, tells his audience that it was not Isaiah alone who foretold the coming of Christ; rather, "To Him all the prophets bear witness" (10:43). This revelation is not at all insignificant. Not only can the whole of Scripture be divided into Law and Gospel, but the whole of Scripture is about Jesus Himself. Not only are Law and Gospel the keys to rightly understanding the written Word of God; they are also the keys to understanding the incarnate Word of God and His divine work. The Lutheran Confessions describe this work by saying that the Law is "a foreign work of Christ, by which He arrives at His proper office, that is, to preach grace, console, and quicken, which is properly the preaching of the Gospel" (Ep V 10).

29. In these passages Paul very clearly and succinctly summarizes the great emphases of Scripture. Men are sinners, but "Christ Jesus came into the world to save sinners" (1 Timothy 1:15). Sin leads to death, but "the free gift of God is eternal life" (Romans 6:23). Sin and salvation, life and death: from Genesis to Revelation the Scriptures consistently highlight this dialectic of Law and Gospel. One exhorts, the other comforts; one chastises, the other consoles; one condemns, the other saves. These dual emphases are illustrated and proclaimed throughout the great sweep of Old Testament history, in the preaching of Christ, in the sermons of Acts, in the Letters of Paul and the other New Testament authors. From this witness of the whole of Scripture—and even in such brief verses as those here read—the reformers were led rightly to believe that "as often as mention is made of the Law and of works, we must know that Christ as Mediator is not to be excluded" (Ap III 251).

30. There are some who believe the Bible to be sort of guidebook to holy living, that is, a book which describes and prescribes what people must do to live a holy life. This is not entirely incorrect; the Law found in Scripture certainly tells us how we are to live. But the author of Hebrews reminds us that, even if we were to expend all of our energy in the observation of the Law, we would remain unable to please God without faith. Thus the confessors write that "these two

things ought always to be understood, namely: First, that the Law cannot be observed unless we have been regenerated by faith in Christ, just as Christ says, John 15, 5: *Without Me ye can do nothing*. Secondly, and though some external works can certainly be done, this general judgment: *Without faith it is impossible to please God*, which interprets the whole Law, must be retained" (Ap III 135). As the Letter to the Hebrews gloriously explains, this faith that is God-pleasing is faith in God's own promises, His Gospel. To read the Bible simply as a book of laws is therefore to misread it. It is also—and most importantly—a book of promises.

Divine Discernment (Connect)

31. Many people, even many Christians, do not properly understand the distinction between Law and Gospel. Not recognizing the difference between the two, many outside of the church regard Christianity as a religion of rules and regulations, of doom and gloom. Even more unfortunately, there are those within the church who remained burdened with a sense of guilt or anxiety because they know they do not measure up to the demanding biblical standard of holiness. Properly understanding the distinction between Law and Gospel, the Christian will realize that this guilt is produced by the Law. He or she will also know—and be greatly comforted to know!—that the message of the Gospel is that our guilt has been removed. Despite any feelings to the contrary, our Lord sees us as perfectly holy, our sins having been covered by the death of His only Son.

32. Many simply open the Bible and begin reading at random. Some read the Bible merely as literature. Others scan the text of Scripture looking for answers to particular questions. Reading God's Word is always to be encouraged. But reading God's Word with an awareness of its two major themes will provide a depth of understanding that many miss. Being aware of the nature and purpose of the Law, readers will gain a deeper understanding of their own nature: creatures made in the image of God but, having fallen into sin, separated from God and standing under His judgment. Being aware of the nature and purpose of the Gospel, readers will gain a deeper understanding of God's own nature: loving, merciful, and forgiving, willing to sacrifice His own Son so that we might once again be united with Him.

Test Your Skills (Vision)

33. As it stands, this comment is not false. The Old Testament does "contain" the Law and the New Testament does "contain" the Gospel. When stated in this simplified manner, however, the impression may be given that these are the only contents of each. The passages listed in question 27 may be appealed to in an attempt to clarify that the Old and New Testaments each contain both Law and Gospel. Were there no Gospel before Christ's incarnation, then Old Testament believers would have been denied salvation. Paul declares, "No one is justified before God by the law" (Galatians 3:11). The author of Hebrews, however, clearly indicates that Old Testament believers will dwell with God in heaven (see Hebrews 11:13–16).

Comparison Chart:

Exodus 20:3—As the First Commandment, this passage is clearly Law.

John 3:16—This verse, of course, is "the Gospel in a nutshell."

Ephesians 2:8–10—That which God provides us because of Christ, namely His unmerited grace and the gift of faith to receive it, is Gospel. God's condemnation of our self-righteous works, as well as the works performed after we have come to faith, are Law.

Leviticus 11:7–8—As ceremonial law, Old Testament food restrictions have been abrogated (abolished) through the coming of Christ (see Matthew 5:17; Acts 10:9–16).

Mark 16:16—The gift of faith and the promises of Holy Baptism are Gospel. Rejecting God's saving gifts and promises through unbelief places one under the Law's condemnation.

Job 19:25–27—Job's expression of expectant hope in his living Redeemer, and his own bodily resurrection, is Gospel.

Luke 22:19–20—The institution of the Lord's Supper, whereby Christ grants us the forgiveness of sins through His broken body and poured-out blood, is Gospel.

1 Timothy 5:23—While Paul's Holy Spirit–inspired words appear to be "sanctified advice," properly speaking they are still Law.

Isaiah 9:6–7—Fulfilled in Christ, Isaiah's ancient prophecy is Gospel.

Hebrews 13:1—The writer's appeal to fraternal charity is Law.

Colossians 3:1–4—Paul faithfully presents the Gospel (see also 2:9–15) as the motivation for the Christian's thankful obedience to the Law.

Applying Law and Gospel

Objectives

By the power of the Holy Spirit working through God's Word, participants will (1) understand the effects of Law and Gospel upon those who hear them, (2) recognize the consequent need for the skillful application of Law and Gospel, and (3) appreciate the graciousness of God, who offers and applies the Gospel in many and various ways.

Opening Worship

Though often thought of as an ordination hymn, "Preach You the Word" (*Lutheran Worship* 259) duly emphasizes the need all Christians have to speak Law and Gospel faithfully, assured that God Himself works through His Word. Likewise, the Collect for the Commemoration of Pastors and Confessors (*Lutheran Worship*, p. 104) offers appropriate thanks for God's having mercifully provided His church with those whose office is proclaiming Law and Gospel.

Focus

34. Read, or ask a participant to read, the first paragraph. Spend some time discussing the ways in our speech can have unintended results and the reasons for this. Encourage participants to share examples from their own lives. Allow them time to consider the circumstances under which their words were misinterpreted. If they are able to remember, let participants explain why it was that they were misunderstood and what they might have said or done to prevent this. Many such misunderstandings are of minor importance; in fact, as an essential part of any situation comedy, they are often a source of amusement. When the words are God's own, however, misunderstanding becomes much more serious.

Completing the Task (Inform)

It is of great importance that Christians properly understand Law and Gospel. It is of equal importance, especially if we are to make disciples of all nations, that Christians be able to articulate and correctly apply God's Word of Law and Gospel. In order to do so, it is necessary to understand not only the nature and purpose of each, but also the effects—intentional and unintentional—that each may have upon their hearers.

35. In spite of unending hardship and persecution, the apostle Paul remained well aware of the apostle's task. It was to be nothing other than "to testify to the gospel of the grace of God" (Acts 20:24). Given the persecution he suffered, Paul could have made his life infinitely more comfortable if he had simply refused to give such testimony. Or he could have given a less controversial testimony. He did not, however, because he was well aware that saving faith is founded upon no testimony other than that of God's gracious Gospel. And, as he explains in his Epistle to the Romans, "Faith comes from hearing" (10:17). For this reason the authors of the Lutheran Confessions note that faithful proclamation of the Gospel is the means by which Christ "collects an eternal Church for Himself. . . . And by this means, and in no other way, namely, through His holy Word, when men hear it preached or read it, and the holy Sacraments when they are used according to His Word, God desires to call men to eternal salvation" (SD II 50).

36. Though the proclamation of the Gospel is the means by which Christ calls men to salvation, this does not mean that there is no necessity of also applying the Law. Jesus, although He Himself would fulfill the Law in His atoning death, tells His audience, "Whoever relaxes one of the least of these commandments and teaches others to do the same will be called least in the kingdom of heaven" (Matthew 5:19). For this reason it is vitally important that we know what God's commandments are, that we know His Law. This is also essential because, if we do not know the Law, we will remain unaware of our sin and our consequent need for salvation. As the psalmist asks, "Who can discern his errors?" (19:12). Unless God's Law itself reveals our sin and accuses us of it, we will remain ignorant of our need for the Gospel. Both Law and Gospel must therefore be applied to Christians and non-Christians alike. The truth of this and the reasons for doing so are emphasized in the reformers' confession that "these two doctrines,

we believe and confess, should ever and ever be diligently inculcated in the Church of God even to the end of the world, although with the proper distinction." The reasons are so that "through the preaching of the Law and its threats in the ministry of the New Testament the hearts of impenitent men may be terrified, and brought to a knowledge of their sins and to repentance" and so that "they be comforted and strengthened again by the preaching of the holy Gospel concerning Christ" (SD V 24–25).

37. The Book of Acts, describing the early growth of the Christian faith, contains a large number of evangelistic sermons. Two examples of such sermons illustrate the manner in which Law and Gospel were applied by early Christian preachers. In chapter 2, Peter recalls the events of Christ's life, death, and resurrection. As he does so, he applies the Law by emphasizing that Christ's death was effected "by the hands of lawless men," (v. 23) including his hearers. But when the Law had done its work, when his audience was "cut to the heart," (v. 37) Peter is quick to apply the Gospel. He encourages them to receive Baptism "in the name of Jesus Christ for the forgiveness of your sins," (v. 38) and he assures them that the Gospel promises have been made even for them and for their children. Peter also applies Law and Gospel in his sermon of chapter 3. He accuses his audience of having "denied the Holy and Righteous One" (v. 14) and "killed the Author of life" (v. 15). But having done so, he also assures them that, with repentance, God will "send the Christ appointed for you, Jesus" (v. 20). He concludes by announcing again that Jesus was raised and sent "to you first, to bless you" (v. 26). These sermons illustrate well the faithful application of Law and Gospel. They also illustrate the emphasis of the Lutheran Confessions that "the two doctrines belong together, and should also be urged by the side of each other, but in a definite order and with a proper distinction" (SD V 15). Peter preaches both. Distinguishing between the two, he first preaches the Law to effect repentance. After the Law has done its work, he then applies the Gospel to comfort and console with the Good News of salvation.

38. In each of these passages essentially the same question is asked. Although the way in which they are phrased betrays something of the mind-sets of those who ask them, each asks about the way of salvation. The answers received by these two men, though, are startlingly different and may at first cause some confusion. The jailer is given what is perhaps the expected answer: "Believe in the Lord Jesus, and you will be saved" (Acts 16:31). This is the Gospel answer; faith

alone, believing in Christ and His promise effects salvation. The young man in Matthew, however, is told to "keep the commandments" (Matthew 19:17). When he claims to have done so, Jesus tells him to sell everything he has. We then read that the young man "went away sorrowful" (v. 22). What accounts for these different answers? Did Jesus really mean to suggest that obeying the Law or selling our possessions is necessary for salvation? Absolutely not! Rather, Law and Gospel are applied as they are appropriate. The jailer was at the point of despair; he had drawn his sword to kill himself; he fell trembling before Paul and Silas. The night's terrifying events had displayed God's mighty power and left him in desperate need of consolation. By way of contrast, the rich young man approached Jesus proudly and completely unaware of his own sinfulness. He was in need of hearing the Law and being made aware of his inability to earn his own salvation. The manner in which Jesus and Paul apply Law and Gospel illustrates the powerful effects of each—and the vital need for not only distinguishing between the two, but also knowing when each needs to be applied. As Luther often wrote, "The Law is to be preached to secure sinners, the Gospel to terrified sinners." This is because "the Law always accuses and terrifies consciences" (Ap IV 38), preparing them for that which will "console, and quicken, which is properly the preaching of the Gospel" (Ep V 10).

39. Paul explains to the Galatians that all who have been baptized into Christ become "heirs according to promise" (3:29). As noted in the previous session, Paul often uses the word *promise* as a synonym for the Gospel itself. In this light it becomes clear that the Gospel is effectively applied to sinners not only in the preaching of God's Word, but also in the administration of Baptism in the name of His Son. Paul also speaks to Titus of our having become heirs on account of this washing and rebirth. Through this application of water and the Word of the Gospel, he writes, Jesus saved us. The Gospel benefits of Baptism are extolled in the Small Catechism, which explains that "it works forgiveness of sin, delivers from death and the devil, and gives eternal salvation to all who believe this, as the words and promises of God declare" (SC IV 6).

40. As the Gospel is revealed and applied in the Sacrament of Baptism, so it is in the Sacrament of Holy Communion. On the night of its institution, Jesus explained the great benefit of this Sacrament. Taking the cup, He told His disciples they were about to receive "My blood of the covenant, which is poured out for many for the

forgiveness of sins" (Matthew 26:28). This forgiveness of sins is the essence of the Gospel. It is for this reason that the Lutheran Confessions can boldly state that "the entire Gospel and the article of the Creed: *I believe a holy Christian Church, the forgiveness of sin,* etc., are by the Word embodied in this Sacrament and presented to us" (LC V 32). Preaching, Baptism, the Lord's Supper: the Lord has left His church many and various means by which the Good News of His salvation is to be applied to sinners seeking consolation. In humble thanksgiving we receive these gifts for our benefit.

41. Cleansing, washing, making holy: all describe the work of the Gospel, the benefits received from Christ's having given Himself up for our sakes. It is, in fact, this work of the Gospel which both brings the church into existence and preserves her until the Lord's return. Therefore the church is urged to purely and continually preach and teach the Gospel of Jesus Christ. Jesus Himself declares that this is the only means by which we remain a part of His church: "If you abide in My word, you are truly My disciples" (John 8:31). At the same time, the church is jealously to guard the pure doctrine of the Gospel, watching out for those who "create obstacles contrary to the doctrine that you have been taught" (Romans 16:17). On the basis of its central place in the church, the authors of the Lutheran Confessions note that the Gospel is the means by which the church can be both recognized and defined. "We know," they write, "that the Church of Christ is with those who teach the Gospel of Christ" (Ap III 279). This, they further explain, relates not only to the preaching of the Gospel, but also to its application in the Sacraments: "The Church is the congregation of saints, in which the Gospel is rightly taught and the Sacraments are rightly administered" (AC VII 1).

Aptly Applied (Connect)

42. We are often unable to discern our own sinfulness. We are also frequently tempted to downplay the consequences of what we may consider to be insignificant faults. That we might never delude ourselves or become self-righteous, God Himself has ordained men to proclaim and to apply the Law, to reveal and announce on the basis of His Word that we are—even if it is not obvious—sinful and deserving of God's wrath. But we may give thanks that this is not the only task for which God has appointed His ministers. They are also to proclaim the Gospel. Though we are often unaware of our sins, we can become

equally forgetful regarding the forgiveness of our sins. For this reason pastors are charged with the task of faithfully and constantly preaching this forgiveness in biblical sermons and applying this forgiveness in the administration of the Sacraments.

43. As the readings in this session illustrate, Law and Gospel are not to be applied randomly or without thought. Consideration must be given to the purpose and effects of each, as well as to the circumstances particular to the hearer. Because the Law is meant to reveal sin and the Gospel to forgive sin, it will be important to apply the one before the other. At times there may even be circumstances under which there is no necessity of proclaiming the Law. Those already conscious of and burdened by their sin will only find relief in the words of God's sure promise of forgiveness for the sake of Christ.

A Faith-Filled Response (Vision)

44. Christians often hear it said—even by fellow Christians—that attendance at services of Word and Sacrament is unnecessary. "After all," it's said, "I can get the same thing from reading my Bible at home." It is certainly true that God's Word contains all that is necessary for salvation. However, there is great benefit in hearing this Word *proclaimed*. For this reason the preaching office was ordained by Christ Himself. Through the work of this office, Law and Gospel are distinguished and applied to the church and her members. What is more, this written and proclaimed Word is not the only benefit God would have His people receive. As a reading of God's Word makes clear, Jesus also instituted the Sacraments by which His Gospel is applied. We come into God's house not because we are coerced by necessity, but because we are eager to receive all of the good gifts there made available for the strengthening and preserving of our faith.

45. Because the Gospel is indeed applied in the Sacrament of the Altar, Luther arranged brief questions and answers as an aid to those preparing for its reception. In a biblical, pastoral manner, Luther first appeals to the Law. "Do you believe you are a sinner?" he asks. "How do you know this?" "What have you deserved from God because of your sins?" As the answers to these questions make clear, it is the Law, summarized in the Ten Commandments, that reveals our sin, its consequences, and our need for the Gospel. This Gospel is then extolled in brief questions regarding Christ's death for the forgiveness of sins and, finally, with respect to the Sacrament itself. Contemplation

of these questions and their answers is an ideal way to spend a few moments, either before worship begins or while you await your turn to approach the altar.

Law, Gospel, and Justification

Objectives

By the power of the Holy Spirit working through God's Word, participants will (1) understand how Christ's birth, life, and death affect the Christian's relationship to the Law, (2) recognize that justification occurs not by the Law, but only through the working of the Gospel, and (3) appreciate the means Christ has instituted to effect and preserve our salvation.

Opening Worship

As "the Gospel in a nutshell" is the most commonly memorized verse of Scripture, this session on justification might begin with a recitation of John 3:16. "Salvation unto Us Has Come" (*Lutheran Worship* 355) marvelously extols God's work of justification, clearly distinguishing between the roles played by Law and Gospel. Having been redeemed through faith in Christ's gracious Gospel, the prayer For Steadfast Faith (*Lutheran Worship*, p. 125) may be prayed together as a humble request that God continue to strengthen and uphold this saving faith.

Focus

46. Read, or ask a participant to read, the first paragraph. Spend some time discussing the ways in which the words *justify* and *justification* are used in everyday conversation. Encourage participants to think of a time when they felt justified in doing something that others may have considered wrong. If they are willing, ask them to explain why they felt so. Quite frequently we attempt to justify our actions by appealing to the law. That is, though we understand why others think we have committed some wrong, we argue that technically—according to the letter of the law—we are innocent.

Just an Observation (Inform)

Though we may often think of *justify* and *justification* as technical theological language, they are in fact derived from the courtroom. They are legal terms. It is not surprising then that even in their theological use they have some relation to the Law. What may be surprising is the way in which the Bible speaks of justification in relation to the Law.

47. Though discussed previously in session 1, the Law's inability to justify deserves mention again. In Galatians 2:15–16 (only two verses!) Paul says three times that justification is impossible according to the Law. He obviously does not want this point to be missed. And just to make sure it is not, he emphasizes this even more strongly again in the fifth chapter, saying that "You are severed from Christ, you who would be justified by the law; you have fallen away from grace" (v. 4). This is no small matter. The Law of God is good and holy; but by it we cannot be made holy. Paul makes this point so strongly and so often that it could not be ignored by the Lutheran reformers. They wrote that because "men by their own strength cannot fulfill the Law of God, and all are under sin, and subject to eternal wrath and death, on this account we cannot be freed by the Law from sin and be justified" (Ap IV 40). But this does not mean that the Law has no place in God's plan for our salvation.

48. Though the Law is powerless to justify, the New Testament is also clear that the Law plays an important role in preparing men for the free gift of justification. St. Paul takes pains to insist that the Law is not opposed to the promises of God. What then is their relationship? Paul explains that "the law was our guardian until Christ came, in order that we might be justified by faith" (Galatians 3:24). Justification is by faith; not Law. But it was the Law which led us to Christ, in whom we place our faith. How did it do this? The accusations of the Law lead sinners to repentance. Concerning this the Lutheran Confessions state that "to repent means nothing else than truly to acknowledge sins, to be heartily sorry for them, and to desist from them. This knowledge comes from the Law" (SD V 8–9). By this function of the Law man is prepared to receive the Gospel. Being made aware of his sins, man is made aware of his need for forgiveness. Thus, the Law is sometimes referred to as God's "alien" work, while the Gospel is called His "proper" work. The confessors make this distinction when discussing the relationship between the Law, the Gospel, and justification: "He

must do the work of another (reprove), in order that He may do His own work, which is to comfort and preach of grace" (SD V 11).

49. All men are born under the Law. Jesus, being true man as well as true God, was not exempted from this condition of birth. Paul makes note of this when he mentions that the Son of God was "born of woman, born under the law" (Galatians 4:4). But, as he also goes on to explain, He was thus born for a particular purpose. He was born under the Law "to redeem those who were under the law" (v. 5). What exactly does the apostle mean by this? Remembering the chief purpose of the Law—to reveal man's sin and to accuse him of his sinfulness—it would not be wrong to say that the Law announces a curse on us. It announces that we who have not fulfilled the Law deservedly face death and condemnation. The good news is that we do not. St. Paul explains the reason for this. "Christ redeemed us from the curse of the law by becoming a curse for us" (Galatians 3:13). Not only was Christ born *like* us, born under Law, but He was also born *for* us, to suffer in our place the curse that had been pronounced on us. Therefore, commenting on Galatians 3:13, the Confessions state that "the Law condemns all men, but Christ, because without sin He has borne the punishment of sin, and been made a victim for us, has removed that right of the Law to accuse and condemn those who believe in Him" (Ap III 58).

50. Christ's relationship to the Law—being born under it and having suffered its curse—radically affects the relationship between Christians and the Law. Though the Law formerly accused us, or, as Paul says, "stood against us with its legal demands," its power to do so has now been nullified. Having both fulfilled the Law and suffered under it, our Lord canceled "the record of debt" (Colossians 2:14). With Christ's very body the Law was taken away and nailed to the cross. We can therefore joyfully confess with Paul that "Christ is the end of the law" (Romans 10:4). We can joyfully confess with the reformers that "since they [Christians] are accounted righteous, the Law cannot accuse or condemn them, even though they have not actually satisfied the Law" (Ap 3.58). That final clause is important. We have not actually satisfied the Law. Our relation to the Law has not changed because of something we have done. It is only on account of Christ and His saving work that the Law no longer accuses or condemns. It is only on account of the Gospel that the curse of the Law has been removed.

51. Jesus' relationship to the Law is intimately entwined with His relationship to the Gospel. While Paul tells the Romans that his Gospel is none other than "the preaching of Jesus Christ" (16:25), he also explains to the Corinthians that the Gospel saves (1 Corinthians 15:2). As he outlines the content of this saving Gospel message, he cannot but mention the central event of the Gospel, that "Christ died for our sins" (v. 3). That is, Christ died because we had broken the Law; Christ suffered the ultimate penalty of the Law's curse. It might be said in a sense that Jesus' relation to the Law *is* the Gospel. The news that he suffered the Law's penalty in our place *is* the good news. This is the point Luther makes as he confesses the doctrine of justification in his famous explanation of the Creed's Second Article: "I believe that Jesus Christ . . . is my Lord, who has redeemed me, a lost and condemned creature, purchased and won me from all sins, from death, and from the power of the devil, not with gold or silver, but with His holy, precious blood and with His innocent suffering and death" (SC II 4).

52. The Colossians are informed that, on account of Christ's death, they have been reconciled to God and can now stand "holy and blameless and above reproach before Him" (1:22). Upon hearing this good news, they are simply informed that this is "the hope of the Gospel" (1:23). Indeed it is! Once being alienated, now being reconciled; once being evil, now being holy; once enemies, now free from accusation: these are the amazing effects of the Gospel of Jesus Christ. These are benefits not to be squandered. Paul therefore urges his audience to continue in their faith, to remain "stable and steadfast, not shifting from the hope of the gospel that you heard" (1:23). Paul's exhortation to the Colossians remains relevant for each of us today. Having been redeemed from the Law and reconciled by the Gospel, let us continue joyfully and thankfully in the faith which lays hold of such good news. We can do so with the assurance that it is God's own Spirit who has "called me by the Gospel, enlightened me with His gifts, sanctified and kept me in the true faith" (SC II 6).

Sons and Heirs (Connect)

53. Christians familiar with both the Scriptures and their own behavior will be acutely aware of their inability to keep the Law. This should never lead one to despair of salvation, however. The good news of the Gospel is that Jesus Himself was born under the Law, that He perfectly fulfilled the Law's demands in His earthly life, and that He

suffered the condemnation of the Law in His atoning death. These things He did in our place, for our sake. This is the Christian's great comfort: all that we cannot do, Christ has done for us.

54. Just as we have been saved through faith in the Gospel of Jesus Christ, so too does the ministry of the Gospel continue to strengthen and preserve our faith. This, in fact, is the reason behind the writing of so many of St. Paul's New Testament Letters. He knows that his audience has received salvation by grace through faith in Christ. In many cases it was Paul himself who first proclaimed the Gospel of Christ to them. Yet he writes to remind them of this Gospel, to comfort, to encourage, and to strengthen the faith of those who already believe. These same benefits are received when we read the Scriptures or hear them proclaimed. Likewise, we receive these benefits through the administration of the Gospel by means of the Sacraments. So long as we remain in this world, afflicted by sin and our lingering sinful nature, we will eagerly seek to make use of these gracious gifts of God.

All about Christ (Vision)

55. As the Scriptures and the Lutheran Confessions frequently make clear, the mingling of Law and Gospel is a dangerous and harmful thing. One way in which they are mingled or confused is by appointing to one the work of the other. To be sure, as we will review in the next session, Christians do follow the Law of God; but this in no way affects the justification which has been freely received by faith in the Gospel of Christ. Perhaps the best response to those who believe that keeping the Law is necessary for salvation is to review with them the numerous passages in which St. Paul declares that the Law cannot justify. Galatians 5:4 is a particularly strong statement on this matter. Galatians 3:3 is also quite relevant; here the Galatians are asked, "Are you so foolish? Having begun by the Spirit, are you now being perfected by the flesh?"

Law, Gospel, and Sanctification

Objectives

By the power of the Holy Spirit working through God's Word, participants will (1) understand the proper distinction between justification and sanctification, (2) recognize a third use of the Law and its relation to Christian sanctification, and (3) appreciate and give humble thanks for the work of God Himself in sanctification.

Opening Worship

You may choose to begin this session with a responsive reading of the Third Article of the Creed and Luther's explanation, titled Sanctification. "Oh, that the Lord Would Guide My Ways" (*Lutheran Worship* 392) is a popular hymn which affirms the Lord's own work in sanctification. As the sanctified life is indeed a new life in Christ, the prayer For Newness of Life in Christ (*Lutheran Worship*, p. 125) is well-suited to opening worship.

Focus

56. Read, or ask a participant to read, the first paragraph. Spend some time discussing the definition of holiness. Ask participants if, in their experience, they have noticed a difference between the way the term is used within the church and the manner in which it is used by non-Christians. If they have, encourage them to suggest reasons why the term may be so unpopular outside of the church. Unfortunately, as some may suggest, it could be that the term has been too frequently misunderstood and misused by Christians themselves.

A Faith That Works (Inform)

Sanctification is perhaps one of the most frequently misunderstood, and therefore hotly debated, topics in the Christian church. As with the interpretation of Scripture and the doctrine of justification, to arrive at a correct understanding of sanctification, it is necessary to properly understand and consistently maintain the biblical distinction between Law and Gospel.

57. James famously declares that "faith apart from works is dead" (2:26). He offers a clear reminder that faith is not the end of Christian life, but its beginning. This does not at all imply that deeds must be added to faith in order to effect our salvation. It does mean, however, that our saving faith is also a sanctifying faith. The faith by which we lay hold of the Gospel promise is also a faith that prompts us to do those works which please God. Indeed, it is only this saving faith that allows us to perform God-pleasing works, works which God Himself has revealed in His Law. Paul explains this while clearly distinguishing between justification and sanctification. Justification, he says, "is the gift of God, not a result of works" (Ephesians 2:8–9). And yet, once being justified, we are freed "for good works, which God prepared beforehand, that we should walk in them" (2:10). The Lutheran reformers likewise distinguish between Law and Gospel, justification and sanctification, when they write that "although men truly believing and truly converted to God have been freed and exempted from the curse and coercion of the Law, they nevertheless are not on this account without Law, but they have been redeemed by the Son of God in order that they should exercise themselves in it day and night" (Ep VI 2).

58. The above point is further clarified in St. Paul's Letter to the church at Rome. Because the Law reveals sin and condemns sin, those who live under the Law are also slaves to sin. But the Christian lives under grace. Paul is quick to point out, however, that our freedom from the Law has not given us a license to sin. Freedom from the Law does not mean complete freedom; the Christian remains a slave, not to sin and the Law, but now to righteousness. It is only as holy slaves to righteousness that we have been freed to obey that which is holy and righteous. While the Law always accuses, in Christ we have been freed to obey and it no longer condemns us. Indeed, those who have been made slaves to righteousness by the working of God's Spirit will eagerly and inevitably walk in the ways of God's holy Law. The Confessions thus explain that "when by faith we have received the Holy Ghost, the fulfilling of the Law necessarily follows" (Ap XX 92).

59. The vocabulary used by the Pharisees offers a striking contrast to that used by Jesus. The Pharisees asked Jesus accusingly, "Why do Your disciples break the tradition of the elders?" (Matthew 15:2). Jesus replied by asking why the Pharisees break "the

commandment of God" (v. 3). Indeed, he says, they break God's command for the sake of tradition. By doing so they have become guilty of nullifying God's Word for the sake of human traditions. Some human traditions may certainly be useful and good. But they do not have the status of commandments, and they must never supplant God's commandments. The New Testament refers quite harshly to those who suggest otherwise, calling them insincere "liars" (1 Timothy 4:2) who follow "deceitful spirits and teachings of demons" (v. 1). The authors of the Lutheran Confessions warn against such teachings by explaining that the "doctrine of the Law is needful for believers, in order that they may not hit upon a holiness and devotion of their own, and under the pretext of the Spirit of God set up a self-chosen worship, without God's Word and command" (SD 6.20). Our sanctification is not a matter of self-chosen good works; it is rather a matter of those works to which God Himself exhorts us and which His Holy Spirit works in us to fulfill.

60. Psalm 119 is a beautiful meditation on the Law of God. In it the psalmist expresses his love of God's Law and his desire to walk in its ways. Given our understanding of the first and second uses of the Law, this may at first seem strange. Surely none delight in the coercion, accusation, and condemnation that result from the first two uses. The psalmist understands, however, that the Law has yet another use. The Formula of Concord notes this third use in saying that "the Law of God is useful, 1. not only to the end that external discipline and decency are maintained by it against wild, disobedient men; 2. likewise, that through it men are brought to a knowledge of their sins; 3. but also that, when they have been born anew by the Spirit of God . . . they live and walk in the Law" (SD 6.1). As a revelation of the will of God—a lamp and a light—it serves as a guide for those who have been redeemed and thus freed to live their lives in accordance with God's will. While it is impossible to please God without faith, the Law teaches those who do have faith how they might by their actions please God in their daily lives. This third use of the Law is therefore an exclusively Christian use of the Law. It is proclaimed to those who have been justified by Christ's Gospel in order that they might know how to "live under Him in His kingdom, and serve Him in everlasting righteousness, innocence, and blessedness" (SC II 4).

61. In discussing sanctification, Paul uses the language of "putting off" and "putting on." Much like the manner in which we change clothes, he says, we have also taken off our old selves and put

on new selves. This new self, he goes on to say, is "being renewed in knowledge after the image of its creator" (Colossians 3:10). Using a different metaphor, Peter speaks of the Christian "being built up as a spiritual house" (1 Peter 2:5). Significantly, both Peter and Paul speak of these processes in passive terms: "being renewed" and "being built." The process of becoming a "holy priesthood" is not something in which the Christian endeavors alone. To the contrary, it is something that God Himself effects; He renews, He builds—He makes holy, that is, sanctifies, according to His will. Indeed, we could not even make a beginning if God Himself were not active in this process. As the reformers wrote, "the Law says indeed that it is God's will and command that we should walk in a new life, but it does not give the power and ability to begin and do it; but the Holy Ghost, who is given and received, not through the Law, but through the preaching of the Gospel, Gal. 3,14, renews the heart" (SD VI 11). For this reason they even distinguish between man's own works done in obedience to the Law and those which result from the Spirit's working in man. They write, "when a man is born anew by the Spirit of God . . . and is led by the Spirit of Christ, he lives according to the immutable will of God comprised in the Law, and so far as he is born anew, does everything from a free, cheerful spirit; and these are called not properly works of the Law, but works and fruits of the Spirit" (SD VI 17).

62. Scripture consistently affirms that, even after his conversion, man neither keeps the Law nor becomes sanctified without God Himself working in and through him. Thus, even Jesus Himself prays to His Father that He may "Sanctify them in the truth" (John 17:17). Likewise, Paul assures the Philippians that the God who justified them will also sanctify them; he writes that "He who began a good work in you will bring it to completion" (1:6). And again he assures them that "it is God who works in you, both to will and to work for His good pleasure" (2:13). Though the work of God in sanctification is sometimes overlooked in contemporary Christianity, it was not neglected by the authors of the Lutheran Confessions. Recognizing that "the Law cannot be kept without Christ; and likewise the Law cannot be kept without the Holy Ghost" (Ap III 5–6), they were led to joyfully confess that it is the Holy Ghost who "has called me by the Gospel, enlightened me with His gifts, sanctified and kept me in the true faith" (SC II 6).

63. Paul's confession to the Romans is a powerful one. He desires to do the will of God, yet he is unable to do so. He agrees with the

Law, but his sinful nature will not allow him to fulfill it. He therefore reminds the Philippians that even he cannot say "that I have already obtained this or am already perfect" (3:12). Because sin still clings to even those redeemed by Christ, the sanctified life is not a life of perfection. That is, sanctification will never be completed on this side of heaven. The reformers thus confess that "believers are not renewed in this life perfectly or completely . . . for although their sin is covered by the perfect obedience of Christ . . . nevertheless the old Adam clings to them still in their nature and all its internal and external powers" (SD VI 7). They likewise condemn the opinion that "a Christians who is truly regenerated by God's Spirit can perfectly observe and fulfill the Law of God in this life" (Ep XII 25). Though we are assured by the Gospel that God Himself has *declared* us perfectly holy and sees us as such, we will not be *made* so until our bodies are transformed in His heavenly presence.

64. A misunderstanding of sanctification, being a misunder- standing of Law and Gospel, is no small matter. Calling them foolish and bewitched, Paul strongly chastises the Galatians for such a misunderstanding. He asks them bluntly, "Having begun by the Spirit, are you now being perfected by the flesh?" (3:3). Or, put another way, he asks if they began with the Gospel only to turn then to the Law. The folly of doing so is pointed out by indicating that the Holy Spirit does not work among them because they obey the Law, but only on the basis of their faith. Taking up the practical example of circumcision, the apostle again warns against trusting in one's ability to obey the Law. The Christian, while continuously being sanctified by the Holy Spirit, will never take confidence in his or her ability to fulfill the Law. Rather, we say with Paul, "But far be it from me to boast except in the cross of our Lord Jesus Christ" (Galatians 6:14). It is in the Gospel of the cross that our justification has been announced and our sanc- tification begun.

Saint and Sinner (Connect)

65. Because we are incapable of effecting our own salvation, it is a great consolation to know that we are not responsible for our own salvation. The same is no less true of sanctification. Though we have put off the old self and put on a new, even this new self remains unable to fulfill the Law. It is greatly comforting to know, then, that we are not left to fulfill the Law of our own power. Instead, Christ prays that

the Father Himself sanctify us by means of His Word. The apostles Peter and Paul also assure us that another is at work in us, renewing us and building us into a holy—that is, a sanctified—priesthood. Our sinfulness, therefore, is no cause for despair. It is cause for us ever more thankfully to take hold of God's promises, the promise of what He has done on the cross and the promise of what He continues to do in our daily lives.

66. Christians who honestly assess their life and works are forced to confess that they are not perfect, that their actions are not in accordance with the Law, and that they even do many things contrary to their own desires. Though this continuing sinfulness is cause for great sorrow, it is some small comfort to know that our struggle against sin is not unique; even the great St. Paul was not free from sin. But Paul's lifelong battle with the flesh provides comfort not only because "misery loves company," but because he offers an exemplary illustration of how the Christian is to respond to his or her own sinfulness. Like Paul, we will freely and humbly acknowledge and confess our sin, give constant thanks for Christ's free justification, and pray for the Holy Spirit's ongoing work of sanctification.

Christ in Action (Vision)

67. The claim that God justifies man while man sanctifies himself is often made in an attempt to simplify the distinction between the doctrines of justification and sanctification. Unfortunately, this is an *over*simplification that inadvertently subverts the work of the triune God. God alone is indeed responsible for declaring us holy. But He is not complacent in the process of our being made holy. The indwelling of His Holy Spirit stirs up in the Christian a new love of the Law and a desire to keep the Law. But if it were not for the continual working of this Spirit within us, we would remain helpless to work out our sanctification. A review of some of the passages found in previous questions may help clarify that God, in His great mercy, has not redeemed us only to leave us to our own devices. Instead, through the means by which He first called us unto Himself, He continues to work in us, renew us, and transform us into the holy people we were first created to be.

68. There are some who do not believe in a third use of the Law. Some also believe that, since Christ has cancelled the written code, even the second use of the Law, which acts as a mirror to show us our

sins, need not be preached to Christians. Christ did indeed fulfill the Law and nullify its accusatory power. Yet, as even a cursory reading of the New Testament Letters reveals, the earliest Christian authors did not shy away from proclaiming the Law to their (Christian!) audiences. The first letter to the Corinthians illustrates this well. Though Paul rebukes the Corinthians for numerous sins, he never insinuates or implies that they are less than redeemed brothers and sisters in Christ. Paul understood that Christians remain, in the words of Luther, "at the same time saint and sinner." Through the preaching of the Law, we too are reminded of our sinfulness. Being thus reminded, we are encouraged to cling ever more dearly to the sure promise of the Gospel, the power of God for our salvation—and for our continual sanctification.

Appendix of Lutheran Teaching

The Augsburg Confession of 1530

Philip Melanchthon, a lay associate of Dr. Martin Luther, wrote the Augsburg Confession to clarify for Emperor Charles V just what Lutherans believed. Melanchthon summarized Lutheran teaching from the Bible and addressed the controversies of the day. This confession remains a standard of Lutheran teaching.

Article IV

Also they teach that men cannot be justified before God by their own strength, merits, or works, but are freely justified for Christ's sake, through faith, when they believe that they are received into favor, and that their sins are forgiven for Christ's sake, who, by His death, has made satisfaction for our sins. This faith God imputes for righteousness in His sight. Rom. 3 and 4. (*Concordia Triglotta,* p. 45)

Apology of the Augsburg Confession

Philip Melanchthon also wrote an Apology, or "Defense" of the Augsburg Confession to further demonstrate, this time at greater length, the soundness of Lutheran beliefs and practices. Like the Augsburg Confession, the Apology remains a standard of Lutheran teaching.

Article IV 5

All Scripture ought to be distributed into these two principal topics, the Law and the promises. For in some places it presents the Law, and in others the promise concerning Christ, namely, either when [in the Old Testament] it promises that Christ will come, and offers, for His sake, the remission of sins, justification, and life eternal, or when, in the Gospel [in the New Testament], Christ Himself, since He has appeared, promises the remission of sins, justification, and life eternal. Moreover, in this discussion, by Law we designate the Ten Commandments, wherever they are read in the Scriptures. (*Triglotta,* p. 121)

Article IV 43

But since justification is obtained through the free promise, it follows that we cannot justify ourselves. Otherwise, wherefore would there be need to promise? [And why should Paul so highly extol and praise grace?] For since the promise cannot be received except by faith, the Gospel, which is properly the promise of the remission of sins and of justification for Christ's sake, proclaims the righteousness of faith in Christ, which the Law does not teach. Nor is this the righteousness of the Law. For the Law requires of us our works and our perfection. But the Gospel freely offers, for Christ's sake, to us, who have been vanquished by sin and death, reconciliation, which is received, not by works, but by faith alone. (*Triglotta,* p. 133)

Formula of Concord

Following Luther's death in 1546, confusion disrupted the Lutheran churches. Some wished to compromise on matters of doctrine in order to attain greater peace and unity with Calvinists and Roman Catholics. Others claimed to be true Lutherans but strayed from Luther's teaching. In 1576 Elector August of Saxony called a conference to clarify the issues. The result was the Formula of Concord (*concord* means "unity"), published in 1580.

Epitome V 6

But if the Law and the Gospel, likewise also Moses himself [as] a teacher of the Law and Christ as a preacher of the Gospel are contrasted with one another, we believe, teach and confess that the Gospel is not a preaching of repentance or reproof, but properly nothing else than a preaching of consolation, and a joyful message which does not reprove or terrify, but comforts consciences against the terrors of the Law, points alone to the merit of Christ, and raises them up again by the lovely preaching of the grace and favor of God, obtained through Christ's merit. (*Triglotta,* p. 803) (Epitome V is devoted entirely to the discussion of Law and Gospel.)

Solid Declaration V 1

As the distinction between the Law and the Gospel is a special brilliant light, which serves to the end that God's Word may be rightly divided, and the Scriptures of the holy prophets and apostles may be properly explained and understood, we must guard it with especial care, in order that these two doctrines may not be mingled with one another, or a law be made out of the Gospel, whereby the merit of Christ is obscured and troubled consciences are robbed of their comfort, which they otherwise have in the holy Gospel when it is preached genuinely and in its purity, and by which they can support themselves in their most grievous trials against the terrors of the Law. (*Triglotta,* p. 951) (Solid Declaration V is devoted entirely to the discussion of Law and Gospel.)

Glossary

antinomianism. The belief that Christians are free from many, if not all, of the constraints of moral law as recorded in the Bible.

elect. From the Latin for "to choose." Even before He created the world, God chose ("elected") those whom He will save in Christ. The doctrine of election is a comforting doctrine to all who trust in Christ for salvation (see **predestination**).

evangelical. Literally, "good news"—the Gospel. This term is often used to describe churches that stress the Gospel of Jesus Christ in their teachings, especially His death and resurrection to save people from their sin and grant them eternal life.

fundamentalism. A reactionary movement against liberalism and modernism that focuses on certain cardinal tenets of the Christian faith—biblical inerrancy among them—often to the exclusion of other beliefs. Liberal Christians often accuse those believing in biblical inerrancy of being "fundamentalists."

Gospel. The message of Christ's death and resurrection for the forgiveness of sins, eternal life, and salvation. The Holy Spirit works through the Gospel in Word and Sacrament to create and sustain faith, and to empower good works. The Gospel is found in both the Old and New Testaments.

Gospel reductionism. Using the Gospel to suggest considerable latitude in faith and life not explicitly detailed in the Gospel. Associated with liberal Christianity, Gospel reductionism is closely aligned with **antinomianism** and **partial inspiration**.

grace. Properly, God's good will and favor, in and through Jesus Christ, toward sinners, who can plead no merit or worthiness. Scripture also refers to grace in the sense of a gift possessed by humans.

holy. Set apart for a divine purpose (e.g., Holy Scripture is set apart from all other types of writing). The Holy Spirit makes Christians holy (see **sanctification**).

inerrancy. The teaching that the Bible, as originally inspired by the Holy Spirit and recorded by the prophets, apostles, and evangelists, did not contain errors. Churches teaching biblical inerrancy recognize that scribes and translators may have erred in copying the Bible over the centuries.

inspiration. Guidance by a spirit. In many religions the term describes a trancelike state of spirit possession. In Christianity the term usually describes the guidance of God's Holy Spirit provided to the prophets and the writers of the Bible (plenary inspiration; see **verbal inspiration**).

justification. God declares sinners to be just or righteous for Christ's sake; that is, God has imputed or charged our sins to Christ, and He imputes or credits Christ's righteousness to us.

Law. God's will, recorded in His Word, which shows people how they should live (e.g., the Ten Commandments) and condemns their sins. The preaching of the Law is the cause of contrition, or genuine sorrow over sin. The Law must precede the Gospel, otherwise sinners will be confirmed in unrepentance. Like the Gospel, the Law is found in both the Old and New Testaments.

legalism. Legalism can be (1) seeking salvation from God through obedience to God's commands; (2) emphasizing the Law so that the Gospel's proper role is depreciated or excluded; (3) over-stressing the letter, but not the spirit, of the Law.

partial inspiration. Theologically liberal Christians hold different views of the Bible's inspiration. Some assert that the Bible is God's Word but contains factual errors. Others say that the Holy Spirit helps people today determine which parts of the Bible to follow. Others maintain that the Bible is but one of many testimonies to God's Word, including writings of other religions. Still others hold that only those verses in the Bible specifically dealing with the Gospel are inspired (see **Gospel reductionism**).

polemical. From the Greek word for "battle." The term describes conversation or writing that attacks and refutes.

predestination. The act of God whereby He chose those who will be saved in Christ (the "elect"). Calvinists/Presbyterians teach the unbiblical doctrine of double predestination, maintaining that in addition to the elect, God also chose the remainder of humanity for damnation (see **elect**).

sacrament. Literally, "something sacred." In the Lutheran church a sacrament is a sacred act that (1) was instituted by God, (2) has a visible element, and (3) offers the forgiveness of sins earned by Christ. The sacraments include Baptism, the Lord's Supper, and

Absolution (if one counts the person speaking absolution as the visible element; Large Catechism IV 74; Apology XIII 4–5).

sanctification. The spiritual growth that follows justification by grace through faith in Christ. Sanctification is God's work through His means of grace: Word and Sacrament.

verbal inspiration. The Holy Spirit guided the prophets, evangelists, and apostles in writing the books of the Bible, inspiring their very words while using their particular styles of expression. Conservative Christian churches hold that the Bible's words are God's Word and that the original manuscripts of Scripture were without error (see **inerrancy**), but some mistakes may have entered the text as it was copied, edited, or translated over the centuries.

will. After the fall humanity is able to exercise free will in temporal matters. However, in spiritual matters, we are spiritually dead (Romans 8:6–7; Ephesians 2:1) and can neither cooperate with nor make a decision to follow God. Our salvation, the forgiveness of our sins, the cleansing of our soul, and the turning of our will toward God is solely the work of the Holy Spirit (1 Corinthians 12:3; 2 Timothy 1:9) through the Gospel (see **Gospel**).